The Career Change Guide: Dream Job

The Career Change Guide:
How to Find Your Dream Job

V.P. Sarin

MegageM

Published by Megagem Sapience
www.megagem.org
gem@megagem.org

ISBN-13: 978-8190889438
ISBN-10: 8190889435

Manufactured in the United States of America

Contents

		Page
Preface		9
1. Putting Career Change Into Perspective		11
2. Is It Time To Change?		15
3. The Career Change Process		18
4. Assess Yourself — To Discover Your Hidden Drivers		26
5. Explore Careers — To Discover Your True Calling		53
6. Tools & Techniques — To Get The Job You Want		66
7. Job Search — Ways to Your Dream Job		88
8. Employing Yourself — Planning Your Business		104
9. Take Charge		132

List of Illustrations

		Page
1.	Career Change: The Five-Step Process	19
2.	Career Change Vision Statement	23
3.	Work Values Worksheet	33
4.	Fundamental & Self-management Skills Worksheet	37
5.	Work Content Skills Worksheet	39
6.	Identifying Real Talents	39
7.	Identifying Skill Deficiencies	40
8.	Occupational Interests: Exploring Themes	42
9.	Occupational Interests: Exploring Situations	44
10.	Personal Traits Inventory	47
11.	Self-Assessment Summary Sheet	50
12.	Career Selection Worksheet	60
13.	Exploring Preferred Career Domain	63
14.	Exploring Preferred Work Environment	64
15.	Job Search Programme	77
16.	Job Evaluation Worksheet	78
17.	Appraising New Job Offer	86
18.	Direct Employer Contact– Status Report	95
19.	A Comparison of Job Search Methods	102
20.	Planning against Business Failures Worksheet	120
21.	A Standard Business Plan Outline	123

Preface

Career is a major part of our active life, as it consumes more than half of our waking time. Career plays a vital role in our overall well-being. It also defines who we are, viz., our social standing. Yet, we do not follow a structured approach to manage our career issues. We rely on our self-opinionated attitude or prefer trial-and-error methods to take career decisions.

There is a difference between a career and a great career. There are individuals with almost similar profiles, but at vastly different standings on the success scale. We often come across individuals with virtually same qualifications, experience and skill-sets; but their career positions are poles apart. We cannot brush aside such variations by simply blaming the favourite whipping boy, the luck factor.

Ordinary people rarely review their career plans. They rarely revise their career goals. You are not an ordinary person, as you have already taken the first step aimed at upgrading yourself. You know that you are different from the lot. You have the potential to achieve a great deal in your career. But, having potential and realizing it optimally are two different things. Potential is within you, and it is for you to make best use of it.

The basic premise of the Career Change Guide is that we all have the potential to influence our career success, and we ought to make the best use of our potential. The objective of the book is to make you career conscious, to help you to take charge of your future career, and get the job of your dreams. While studying this book, you will discover parts of you, you never knew existed. The purpose of the book is to enable professionals to create a dynamic career plan and empower them to realize it. And in their career journey, it is intended to help them– all the way in all the ways.

Professional-progress and personal-progress ought to progress together. But, more often than not, personal-progress takes a backseat. We are surely for the professional empowerment, but not at the expense of self-factors. Professional success has no meaning if you are not happy or cannot make others happy. It is not an either/or choice between career success and happiness. The right career strategy aims at a synergistic approach to seek the both. It expects us to clear the decks at the conceptual level. Otherwise, our unbridled quest for success would only drag us deeper into career dilemmas.

This book provides you enough inputs to enable you to effectively deal with your career dilemmas so that you can smartly monitor the future to facilitate the professional and personal progress. You just have to join the dots to figure out the way forward from your career crossroads to your dream career.

I dedicate this book to my professional friends who pestered me to bring out a career change guide based on "Taking the Challenge of Career Change" part of my career-planning book Vision Revision. The credit for many features aimed at enhancing the psychological impact of the material, many times even at the expense of syntax, goes to them who have tested this material and offered invaluable feedback and suggestions to make this work more practical and useful. The mandate I have followed is not to aim at an interesting read, but to take care of your career interests. The objective is to ensure that it empowers you to manage your career successfully and that you are amply motivated to take your career decisions intelligently.

In the career jungle, you have the options to either perish professionally or play your part proficiently. It is up to you to just survive, or strive to thrive.

V.P.Sarin

1. Putting Career Change Into Perspective

We all know that choosing a career is a very important decision of our life, perhaps next only to choosing a spouse. Unfortunately, both offer enough scope to err. And here, choosing not to choose is not a choice. Pretermitting is not the way out of this quandary. Dilly-dallying has its own downsides, to be precise, it slowly but surely takes away some of our competitive and perceived advantages. What's more, the importance of these choices does not diminish in view of whether it is a first career/spouse or the next one.

So, when we know that these choices are so important that our wrong choice can be our undoing, why do many of us make these crucial choices casually and callously? Why do educated and illiterate fare equally on this scale? Why education does not play a significant role in improving the success rate in such crucial choices? Can we absolve ourselves by simply putting the blame on the destiny, usually the pet scapegoat? Or is it our delusive sense of sagacity and know-it-all approach to blame?

Then again, why do we humans suffer more than other creatures when such important choices go wrong? The main things that separate us from the animals are education and marriage. Can we blame these institutions? Or can we point the finger at the God-gifted better brain and blame our special ability to think as a causative factor? Or is it that the animals do not have the similar social context? But then, we ought not to suffer on account of a better brain or a better social system.

We suffer more when we buckle under animalistic tendencies, which prevent us to make the rational use of our God-given abilities. Besides, we often tend to further compound the problem by usually sticking to our wrong choice for quite some time, whereas animals quickly accept their folly and move on, as they do not suffer from the swelled head. Let us shed some light on this predicament with reference to the comparable and equally important decision of marriage to exemplify the importance of choosing a right partner/career.

The Anatomy of a Career Change Decision

We know that choosing a career and choosing a spouse are two equally important and analogous decisions. Yet, we often underestimate the importance and implications of a career change and fail to treat it fairly. Besides, we fail to benefit from the process of choosing a partner that presents an interesting analogy to the anatomy of a career change decision.

Amongst all creatures, only humans have the institution of marriage. Whether it is a blessing or a curse depends on many factors. The most important factor is how we enter this institution. It has a weighty bearing on what we experience subsequently— a heavenly living or a psychic trauma. Put differently, how we decide to marry, that is, basically how we choose our life partner determines whether we will enjoy the matrimonial bliss or endure the shackles, if separation is not the option. And while separation may be a blessing in disguise for many, it cannot be termed as a positive development in general. So, essentially the selection process, i.e., how we choose, influences the outcome. But then, why we cannot lay down the foolproof guidelines or perhaps have an academic course to equip ourselves for such important life-shaping if not lifesaving decisions given that we have the brain and proficiencies to do that. Perhaps we could not earnestly try it owing to our overindulgence in the rat race and other so-called mercenary tasks. So in the absence of any infallible guidelines or standard yardsticks, we often take such important decisions on our own, thanks to our self-involved attitude akin to a rat participating in the rat race. Now, let us explore how and why our choices go wrong.

When a boy selects a girl to marry because she is beautiful, brainy, levelheaded, well bred and rich, it is an objective decision that can be termed as a calculated move. And when the same boy selects a girl because she loves him and/or he loves her, it is a subjective decision based on a prejudice. In the first case, knowledge plays a decisive role. Human factors are responsible for the second decision, perhaps making him an uxorious husband until harsh realities of life dawn on him.

The God has presented us knowledge and human feelings, expecting a rational use of our wisdom to ably determine compatibility quotient while choosing a spouse or a career. That is why when the same boy rationally chooses a girl based on the man and material factors, his chances of success in the marriage are greatly enhanced, and he can look forward to revel in the role of an uxorious husband forever. Similarly, when we take career change decisions after necessary objective considerations in addition to assessing our true love for the new career, it assures much better outcomes. For that reason, in the career change process, our approach will be to draw on the synergy of mind and heart to establish the right blend of objective and subjective parameters to improve our chances of finding a compatible career.

Decision-making process for choosing a life partner and a career is fundamentally the same. And the outcomes of these choices follow the similar pattern as well. However, the process of choosing a spouse is more complex and intense as compared to choosing a career, again probably due to the interplay of our animalistic instincts in the case of former, ostensibly in quest of a true love. Choosing the first career or a new career is relatively simple and simply calls for a sensible approach to reap the rich dividends.

Career change is the topic that usually enervates the rational thinking power of nearly all who think about it compulsively. And it is not a walk in the park, even for those who contemplate it rationally. Yet, career change has become a way of life for the career conscious white-collar people. Many of them are actively seeking a new calling, because they are not genuinely happy with their current career, a fact established by several studies and surveys. Nowadays even the blue-collar people frequently think about a career change because of similar reasons. Predictably, the professionals, who have started their career without a sensible career planning, crave for a career change. Some people who just drift into a career under gratuitous pressure from elders or other temptations equally yearn for a change. Furthermore, earlier very few people had access to the career planning tools and as such, many made the fundamentally wrong career choices. As a result, they deprived themselves the opportunity to exploit their inherent abilities to achieve the success they rightly deserve. In fact, the outdated traditional wisdom against changing careers has been gradually changing. Most people do not consider it relevant to today's workplace. But then, present day employees are usually ingenious as well as ingenuous, which makes them vulnerable while mooting a changeover in this rapidly changing world of work, where the velocity of change itself is dramatically changing.

As it is human nature to tread the path of least effort, people tend to repeat the same mistake of impulsively choosing an inapt career. They do not appreciate the importance of the right career planning to ensure a gratifying and good-fit career. Many people do not even realize that a good fit career is much more important than a good fit dress or shoes. They buy their shoes in a planned way, as they know that bad-fit shoes hurt. But a bad fit career hurts much more as well as adversely affects our work-life balance. And we cannot discard it so easily. Even while changing career direction, i.e., a new career field, many people tend to disregard the importance of a comprehensive and judicious career planning. They often confuse changing career direction with changing employer, which is relatively a simple shift that too in the known territory. As a result, they again land up in an incompatible career line and then once again desperately crave for another career change. Therefore, it is always better to follow a structured approach while changing careers in order to discover the elusive dream career.

2. Is It Time to Change

Career is a major part of our active life, as it consumes more than half of our waking time. Career plays a vital role in our overall well-being. It also defines who we are, namely, our social standing. In spite of this, we do not follow a structured approach to manage our career issues and rather stick to the trial-and-error methods to take career decisions. Besides, our self-opinionated attitude towards our career issues adds to the career dissatisfaction.

It is important that if you are not enjoying a fulfilling and satisfying professional life, you must take charge of your career management immediately. Working at something unsatisfying is an inexcusable excuse to continue the misuse of your true potential. This can upset not only your career and health, but also other aspects of your life. Prolonged frustration at work is self-consuming. But then, frustrations owing to acquisitive tendencies should not play a major role in your decision. So, first and foremost you need to find out what you want your career to achieve, and what you should do to achieve that. It is very important to find what you truly want out of your career and then go all-out to get what you truly want. Remember, your approach will define how good you are at achieving that.

But then, changing a career is not a cinch and as such, a change should not be contemplated without any real and serious reason. It is irrational to change career just for the sake of some money or due to our incongruous personal perceptions. We must bear in mind that most career changes occur because people mismanage their careers. While choosing a career, they often fail to take a well-informed and well-considered decision, and thus lay a foundation for a future career change. On the other hand, it may be the time for a career change if you are enduring three or more of the following incitive situations:

> Experiencing a declining trend in commitment
> Experiencing a declining trend in self-esteem
> Experiencing a declining trend in contribution
> Experiencing: Career fatigue/ Frequent fagged feelings/ Career decay
> Experiencing: Irritability/ Monotony/ Dysphoria
> Experiencing lack of: Motivation/Promotional prospects/ Optimism
> Bypassed for a well-deserved promotion
> Bypassed for a scheduled, deserved key assignment
> Bypassed for a well-earned pay increase
> Ignored by seniors
> Ignored by colleagues
> When you are ousted from an important decision making process
> When there is little scope for further growth in the organization i.e. you have touched the glass ceiling
> When your sixth sense tells you that something is amiss or you ought to make a move

Then again, while taking a career change decision, we must ensure that our decision is not swayed by our compulsive or impulsive behaviour. It is not human nature to thoroughly and prudently consider the consequences of our crucial choices beforehand. This vulnerability makes it a compelling case to chart the course of career change even more carefully and cautiously. Though career change is an incomparable and personal process with no decidedly right or wrong ways to manage the changeover, it pays to follow a structured process and time-tested strategies. While the process provides the direction to gain a competitive advantage, the strategies help us to draw on the desirable human instincts as well as suppress the detrimental human instincts.

Before we examine the career change process, it is pertinent to re-examine the decision of changing career yet again from a different and dispassionate perspective. Cutting the clutter of your mind and building clarity on what you really want is very important to succeed in the career changeover. In fact, this step is also a decisive element of the career change process. It is intended to clarify and complement your conviction. On the one hand, it attempts to pre-empt your doubts from spoiling your subconscious by unnecessarily feeding it that the career change may not be good for you. On the other hand, it also reins in the false hopes from unduly affecting your decision.

In order to exemplify this crucial yet basic step, we step back a step and assume that you are still prospecting a career change, preferably in your field. To keep it simple, we further suppose that you are looking at two options— to continue in the present job or look for another similar job. Now, you have to visualize that neither of these options is open to you and you must find other means to recommence your professional life. You are required to constructively and positively brainstorm over this for a reasonable period of time. Do not prejudge it as an irrelevant exercise with no tangible benefits. Our brain optimally lights up when we brainstorm in such a situation, which in turn facilitates the requisite analysis and synthesis. So, introspect honestly in your own interest. Do not try to deceive yourself. Invest your time and energy on this analysis diligently, and wisely, if your career is important to you.

When you are ready with one or more options after reasonably reasoning out, make a list of pros and cons of the new option(s). After a week, examine again these new alternatives along with the previous two and rationally select the best one. If you still want a career change as per your earlier decision or the new option appeals to you more, write down clearly why you want to make this change and read on carefully as an interested student. And if you decide to continue in the present career, you may casually scan the next section just to update your knowledge about the career change process.

3. The Career Change Process

Career change planning is a simple process, yet it gives a definite competitive edge over others who change careers in an arbitrary manner. It may not be as tall an order as it appears if we carefully plan and diligently follow the requisite steps while changing our career. In fact, it is an easy and winning way to ensure a better success rate in all our career endeavours. In spite of that, we usually find the career change process exciting in the initial stages, but in time, our enthusiasm wanes and we tend to dally and dawdle in our campaign towards our goal. We develop a tendency to deceive ourselves by repeatedly raising mundane doubts and excuses. In fact, our trepidations pressurize us to gravitate towards the following common excuses to halt the process.

- I have a family to support. How can I take the risk of changing my career?
- I have lost touch with the field. How can I effectively compete with others?
- My skills and personal profile may not be relevant for any new career.
- My age or career stage is not right to consider a career change.
- I have become used to working in this work environment with my colleagues. How can I adjust in a new work environment?
- Why should I sacrifice security and stability of my present job for an unknown career?

First of all, you need to have a mechanism in place to preclude such common excuses from unreasonably stalling your process in the middle. Therefore, you should make a list of your probable potent points, which may induce you to abandon the process midway. Review all the potential barriers honestly, deal with the real ones, and resolve not to take shelter in the feeble excuses to throw in the towel midway.

The Steps

Now we are ready to discuss the basic steps involved in a career change process. The sequence of steps is important for executives who intend to finally change career lanes or career direction. The career change process encompasses the following five steps, wherein first two are the preparatory steps, which are discussed in detail in this chapter.

Career Change: The Five-Step Process

Priming Yourself for a Persistent Positive Perspective

Creating Your Career Change Vision Statement

Assessing Yourself– Understanding Your Work Values, Interests, Skills, Personality and Personal Mission.

Exploring Careers– Expanding, Narrowing and Prioritizing Your Career Options. Finalizing The Best One Rationally.

Job Seeking Action Plan– Preparing for the Job Search i.e. Perfecting Tools & Techniques, and Finalizing Job-Seeking Strategies.
    OR
Employing Yourself– Understanding the Business Scene, Planning Against a Business Failure and Creating your Business Plan.

Priming Yourself for a Persistent Positive Perspective

"Your attitude determines your altitude", this oft-repeated saying is very relevant to the career change process. While a positive attitude is a basic requirement for success in career, it becomes crucial during the career changeover process. And if you can remain in a positive frame of mind throughout your career change process, you have won half the battle. Actually, it is an absolute must to successfully seize any career opportunity. So, if you want to make a worthwhile career change, make a change in your attitude first. Your attitude may be positive, yet you have to prime yourself to ensure a persistent positive perspective throughout the changeover process.

Whether your decision to seek a new career originates from the proactive factors, like growth aspirations, better financial rewards, urge to optimally exploit skills and talents, etc. or reactive factors, such as health problems, downsizing, inability to cope with new technology/higher-ups/other changes, etc., you must espouse a proactive and positive attitude. Your positive attitude, patience and persistence can give you a decisive competitive lead, not only over other competitors, but also on you and that is crucial to succeed. But then, it may not be easy to maintain a positive attitude all the time particularly for executives' enduring a career plateau. And it is more difficult during the changeover process, because before contemplating a career switch, you were operating in a familiar environment and somewhat static career situation where the fear of unknown was not playing games with you and as such you were free from the career change anxiety.

Now, we all know that emotional quotient is more important for succeeding in life than intelligence quotient. The emotional quotient and attitude are interconnected and interrelated. When we manifest a positive attitude, it not only reinforces our emotional quotient, but also helps us to capitalize on this factor. On the other hand, a negative attitude adversely impacts our emotional well-being, which is a critical factor to succeed, especially while changing the career direction. So you need to work on bolstering your attitude, as there is always room for improvement, no matter at what age or career stage you are.

It is human nature to experience the usual vicissitudes like negative and positive emotional stimuli, while undergoing any transition. It is not easy to understand the complex working of emotions in order to draw on the positives and rein in the negatives. While you cannot control every negative factor, you can surely control your reactions to minimize their impact. And unless you are adequately primed for the demanding process involved in the career changeover, negative factors will impact you more profoundly and can even turn your dreams to dust. On the other hand, a positive mind-set will help you to take any negative outcome as a challenge rather than a setback. It will help you to capitalize on your strengths and market opportunities as well as effortlessly cope with the downturns in the career changeover process and makes it easier to prevent negativity creeping in. So, it is imperative to have a positive mind-set all along in order to find a career that goes well with your career plan. Therefore, you need to first psychologically psych up your psyche during this crucial transition phase, so that ups and downs do not unduly affect your psyche. You can make use of the following guidelines to prop up your attitude. These are particularly important, whenever positivism dwindles.

- Regularly envision where you want to be after 5 years, and visualize that you are on the way to that goal, with attendant perks to perk up your positive attitude. Engage periodically in an honest introspection and commit to self-development to realize your vision. Think realistically about your abilities, and optimistically believe in yourself.
- Remember nothing can trigger a career growth more than a change of perspective. A positive professional perspective is the key to a high career growth trajectory.
- Liberate yourself from the past, especially past setbacks that generate negative feelings. These negative emotions often get in the way of future opportunities. So, you should sidestep the past and concentrate on the possibilities of the future.
- Do not take your career change too seriously. Just strive to make the most of your opportunities and be in control. You need not worry too much about future uncertainties. Worrying is usually an addiction, which inanely dissipates the valuable time and energy. These resources ought to be deployed optimally to deal with the real barriers coming in the way of your goal.
- Perseverance is the key to a successful career change. Changes take time and you need not get disheartened if you do not get positive results soon enough.
- Help others to help yourself. Find and follow that little cue inside you. Facilitating others in realizing their career

goals will help you to pick up the pace in your efforts. It is the most effective way to boost your attitude.

- Since attitude is contagious, stay away from negative news, people, and environment.
- No doubt, career change is a complex and occasionally destabilizing process. Rather than be daunted by this complex process, learn to convert its complexity to your advantage by suitably priming yourself to gain an edge over competition.
- Never take negative responses personally and play down the post-mortems of rejections. Accept setbacks as stepping-stones. You cannot succeed ubiquitously. So, learn to take the rough with the smooth. You need to view a rejection as a justification to learn more about yourself and research more about suitable opportunities.
- Compose a few positive affirmations relating to your career goals and use them frequently to get out of your comfort zone.
- Make a timetable to implement your career change and follow it. You should think, plan and take steps during this period only. Do not disturb your other leisure interests too much.
- Lastly, accept that you cannot be positive forever and as such have a standby contingency plan ready for your pessimistic bouts. Keep a tight rein on such spells by fixing a time limit for such down periods.

Career Change Vision Statement

Your career change vision statement is that transient part of your career plan, which essentially deals with the ensuing transition in your work life. So, it exclusively focuses on making the most of this change in order to optimally realize your career goals. On the other hand, mismanaging it can result in frustrations, causing more barriers on the way that can take away the momentum from your transition drive. Besides, you must remember that the principal objective of this statement is to set right what you perceive to be wrong with your work life as well as accomplish your career dreams. Therefore while making it, you must avoid *resenting* the previous career, *resorting* to short cuts and *resisting* the necessary changes. And you should *reset* your mind-set for new work life, *restart* your campaign without any hang-ups and *revisit* it time and again. Here is your career change vision statement format, which will help you do that.

Career Change Vision Statement

A. My objectives to make this change are:
   ...

B. The reasons that induce me to go for this change are:
   ...

C. I need to take the following steps to realize my career change vision:

Action Plan:	Steps:	Target Date:
...		
.....		

D. I intend to use these resources to facilitate my career change process:

Resources:	Specific Help:
...	
......	

E. I anticipate the following barriers in the change process and I propose the following ways to manage them.

Potential Barriers:	Forestalling Strategy:
....	
.....	

F. How this career change will help me to accomplish my long term career aspiration:

G. Status report of my career change plan:

Your status report should clearly divide and sub-divide the change process in the specific actions, which needs to be periodically monitored to review the actual progress vis-à-vis the planned progress. This step is an extension of step C to facilitate regular monitoring and incorporating suitable modifications as and when required.

If your career change vision statement becomes long, try to make a point-wise synopsis on one page and keep it on the front page of your change folder for ready perusal. Since this step is a bi-directional one, you can revisit it whenever you like. Moreover, you are not required to complete this step in one session. You can also proceed to subsequent steps if you decide to complete it later.

Then again, if your decision to change career stems from the so-called midlife crisis or have roots in the routine career fatigue and frustrations, i.e., something like the career counterpart of the matrimonial 'seven-year-itch', you ought to wait and let this phase pass in order to ensure that you are not changing direction on frivolous grounds. Even if you have an iota of doubt, you must think twice before proceeding because a tearing hurry at this point can be counterproductive. Here you must remind yourself of ubiquitous lean patches in sports, slack seasons in business, wilderness in politics, down periods in general. And if you cannot correctly see through at this point, you will never be able to steer the ship of your career adeptly. So, at this juncture, planned procrastination pays. Usually, we identify procrastination as a negative word. That is why we often fail to appreciate and draw on the power of planned procrastination, which can prove to be a real blessing in disguise in some situations, like this one.

Moreover, changing career is a dynamic process of matching yourself with the right career in the right environment. And you can change direction anyway if that suits your professional interests. As this is one of the most important decisions of your life, you ought to know yourself well as well as your options. This will help you to pursue your career evaluation or exploration in the right direction. Subsequent chapters will enlighten you in a systematic manner on these themes to prepare you for a smooth career shift.

Finally, a right revision of your vision will magnetize your conduct whereby you will attract positive aspects and repel negative aspects to speed up your march to the envisioned success and satisfaction. But then, it is contingent on how you wield your vision magnet. Remember, a career change can be a bed of roses or neuroses.

4. Assess Yourself – To Discover Your Hidden Drivers

In the previous chapter, we have discussed the career change plan outlining the steps necessary to achieve it. The next crucial step in the process of career change is to assess yourself objectively. This will provide you clear insights into your real self, thus enabling you to explore befitting careers. Your self-assessment is not just intended to aptly evaluate the potentially satisfying careers, but it is also designed to help you evolve professionally. Remember you are solely responsible for your career. And finding happiness and success in your career begins with assessing yourself.

Most of you have travelled some distance on your career path. You have reached a stage in your career; it may or may not match your expectations, and it may or may not correspond to your potential. Whatever the case may be, you have invested a prime and energetic part of your professional life in this journey. So, it is not the time for plain post-mortems to check why you could not achieve what you deserve. Rather, it is time for an honest self-assessment with the aim of devising a game plan to make amends for the shortfall, if any, as well as to ensure that you make the most of your remaining work life to achieve what you truly deserve. However, in the course of evaluating your present status, you also need to look at your past objectively and open-mindedly so as to facilitate an honest dialogue with yourself. This will help you to devise a winning strategy for your future life, both professionally and personally.

We all agree that career-development and self-development move together. We also know that self-assessment is the necessary groundwork to embark on a self-development regimen aimed at realizing our professional aspirations. But our self-complacency and 'know-it-all' attitude often come in the way of this important, but not mandatory exercise of appraising ourselves. Even when we realize its importance and start it, our self-love syndrome comes in the way of an honest assessment. Further, an unprejudiced appraisal is not easy in view of the limitations of the human nature. But it is a must before we proceed to explore our career choices. In addition, a diligently done self-assessment will help us *accentuate* our strong points and *attenuate* our weak points intuitively by drawing on the power of our subconscious and thus accelerating our professional progress.

Besides, we have to recognize that we are not simple products; we are very complex, complicated and unique products. Unless we know the specific attributes of this unique product, we cannot take full advantage of it. And knowing all the attributes is not all that simple, because each product is only one of its kinds with unique set of attributes, such as practical or carefree, leading or following, exploratory or accepting, consistent or flexible, conformist or independent and all the rest. Furthermore, these attributes do not usually manifest at the either end of the spectrum; rather, they are invariably somewhere in between with varying permutations and combinations. That is why it is not easy to fathom this product. But then, in the absence of this product knowledge, we cannot beneficially think about its optimal and intended use, i.e., employment in a befitting career. And assessing the essential attributes of this product can enable us to put it to the best use. Moreover, while the product is complex owing to somewhat dynamic attributes, methodically assessing it is not all that difficult, thanks to years of research and experimentation in the area. But unfortunately, many executives do not take their own self-assessment seriously even though they know that self-assessment is crucial to rightly conceive, believe and achieve our career plans.

Why You Should Do It?

Most executives are largely well acquainted with the importance of self-assessment. Yet, they tend to take this step somewhat indolently. In the pulls and pressures of the career jungle, they often ignore the importance of connecting to themselves, understanding their strengths and weaknesses and appreciating their uniqueness. They even play down the purpose of understanding themselves, while taking important career decisions. They boldly and often blindly explore the alternative career options. And that can be really a chancy lapse. In view of that, let us briefly yet responsibly scan the advantages of self-assessment.

- Self-assessment helps you draw a clear picture of who you are. Construing this self-portrait in the context of your career vision will definitely improve your competitive position. Further, this self-knowledge will help you match your strengths and work-life needs with potentially satisfying careers.

- This self-evaluation leads to a realistic, well-directed approach to career exploration. It helps in broadening the career paths initially, narrowing the career course subsequently and finalizing the most suitable career at the deciding stage.

- It empowers executives with an attitudinal renaissance during the career changeover.

- It is an easy 'Do-It-Yourself' exercise. It is practical and costless. Anyone can do it; it is not rocket science. You can independently draw your self-portrait clearly highlighting positives and acknowledging negatives with the intention of optimally managing these. It helps you to discover your true self without reservations, as you are not trying to impress others.

- This approach focuses more on the employability factors, rather than on the employment. The employability quotient is an individual's permanent asset. It emphasizes more on knowing the quality and suitability of the raw material, which is the best way to ensure the quality of outcome.

- It creates an enabling mindset to manage ego and emotions well, which is important, especially during a career change. It also helps to aptly manage anxiety and pressure incidental to the changeover.

- Often we are not what we perceive and believe we are. It enables a rational review of the set, conceived notions about self in order to strengthen the true notions and discard the false ones.
- Our unique attributes have roots in our unique genetic makeup and conditioning. So, it is imperative to appreciate our unique make up to aptly opt for the relatively standard and defined career fields.
- It improves the quality of career decisions by providing valuable inputs and clearing the decks at the conceptual level. It gives you the confidence to explore befitting careers. When you know yourself well, you can aim at a career that suits you most.
- It rightly evaluates the context-invariant, age-invariant and career stage-invariant attributes, enabling you to optimally exploit them to compete successfully in the changeover game.
- Self-cognizance empowers you to wisely manage the phase between envisioning and vision realization. It facilitates optimal harnessing of positive factors to provide a winning edge, especially while changing career lanes. It also mitigates the impact of negative factors, which often come in the way of careful and considered contemplation of new careers.
- It provides an extremely immersive and personally engaging experience to a serious seeker.

The Process

Having refreshed our memory about some benefits of self-assessment, let us discuss the process. Self-assessment is the first fundamental step in the career planning process. It helps us to discover who we really are before we can make up our mind about what we want to be. It helps us to gain an objective understanding of ourselves by creating a distinct profile in our conscious and subconscious mind. This enlightenment process activates our subconscious mind, which in turn contributes to help us clearly capture, who we really are and, what we expect from our career life. It further facilitates us to optimally draw on our work potential by matching our distinct profile to the most suitable career. This disambiguation process can also help us in revising our career vision with the aim of discovering a satisfying career for the rest of our life. Therefore, self-assessment should take place from time to time throughout our work life, because we are continuously changing and developing.

Now, we take up the main and relevant components of the self-assessment. With an eye to explore potentially rewarding and gratifying career, we need to fully understand what is important to us, i.e., our values; what we are good at, i.e., our skills and talents; what we enjoy, i.e., our interests; and what type of a person we are, i.e., our personality. Hence, self-assessment is the process of taking inventory of our work values, skills & talents, interests, personality and our other personal considerations influencing our career. It is an essential step in the career optimization endeavour. Let us shed some practical light on these important components.

Here it is relevant to mention that when you start something new or absorb something known in a different way, you run the risk of developing a casual and callous approach leading to a passive, careless scanning of the matter. So, please do not give in to the temptations to rush through any exercise or step. Also resist the urge to reply based on 'what you ought to do' rather than 'what you do'. You have to be ruthlessly frank. You should not skip any step even if you feel it is irrelevant. Bear in mind that some exercises meant to acquaint you with your true self may possibly overwhelm you. This is all part of the learning process. Take it in your stride. You should not emotionally identify yourself with the exercise, but should instead activate rational self-reflection so as to ensure a critical as well as encouraging assessment of the self. And be prepared to spend some quality time on this exercise to achieve better results. Many steps aim at priming yourself psychologically to enable you to rightly choose a career that fulfils your known needs as well as little known wants. Therefore, you need to leisurely absorb every step and reflect on it from your personal perspective before finalizing your response. Keep in mind that it is not just the outcome, but how you do these exercises that will determine the contribution of the self-assessment process in your career evolution and career change game plan.

Work Values

It is very important to understand and appreciate your work related values. It will help you to clarify what is really important to you that you must seek in your new career. We all have varied work values, which are essentially the personal motivations or incentives necessary for a satisfying work life. Understanding our work values can help us to take right career decisions. Here are some examples of the ordinary work values.

» Preference for intellectual stimulation at workplace
» Need for security and stability
» Value of financial rewards
» Desire for autonomy at workplace
» Liking for social interaction/ public contact
» Preference for variety in work or repetitive work, and the like

These typical questions are just meant to explain the basic difference between work values and other components of the self-assessment process as well as to initiate your logical thinking on your set of work values. You should bear in mind that your set of work values is incomparable and as such adopting any standard set of work values or copying others work values will not serve your purpose. So, you need to explore your own set of work values. You have to ensure that these values are in harmony with your future professional life in order to realize your career goals. The right work values will not only change your career, but will also have a favourable impact on your work-life balance. And knowing your own set of work values will help you immensely in making prudent career choices.

After appreciating the importance of work-related values, now you need to acquaint yourself with your core work values. Clarifying these in an impartial and receptive manner is a good exercise for any person seeking a career change. This exercise will help you to relate to what is genuinely important to you in your career by identifying your real, true work values. This in turn will help you to choose a potentially satisfying career based on your preferred work values.

Clarifying Your Work Values

The following worksheet will help you clarify your work values. Here are the directions to complete your work values worksheet.

> Add 5 other work values that are important to you and are not included in the list. (Optional step, but desirable)
> You have to rate 35 work values (30 if step 1 is skipped) on a scale of 1 to 5. Ticking ✓in the column 5 implies you consider this particular value most important (vital) and ticking in the column 1 means this is the least important to you (trivial).
> You may select any one number from 1 to 5 for each value and mark ✓ with pencil in the appropriate column adjacent to the value.
> You have to select seven values (six if step 1 is skipped) in all the columns from 1 to 5 i.e. seven ticks ✓ in each column. This limit is intended to place your choices in relative and proper perspective.
> You may change your selection as many times as you like.
> You may select any number for any value, maybe the same number for some contradictory values like financial rewards and career security, working independently and working in a group and the like.

Work Values Worksheet
(Ratings scale: 1=trivial/least important...to...5= vital/most important)

WORK VALUE	Trivial 1	2	3	4	Vital 5
Pay & Perks					
Career Advancement					
Working Independently					
Public Dealings					
Decision Making					
Respect /Status					
Career Continuity/ Security					
Diversity in Work					
Systematic Working					
Exploring Ideas					
Multitasking					
Working Under Pressure					
Assisting People					
Intellectual Stimulation					
Contribution to the Society					
Flexible Schedule					
Formal Environment					
Casual Environment					
Learning New Things					
Meeting Important People					
Authority/ Command					
Personal Achievement					
Working in a Group					
Competence Recognition					
Self Development					
Outings/ Travel					
Serene Work Environment					
Normal Work Hours					
Moral Values					
Physically Active					... >>

31.					
32.					
33.					
34.					
35.					

Now you are in a position to decide the vital and important sets of work values, which you believe can help you realize your professional vision.

A. Vital Work Values: Preferably, without referring to the above worksheet, list seven most important work values that you consider conclusive, i.e., the values deserving 5 or more marks. Column for indicating scores seems superfluous, but can be used to make a distinction within the category, e.g., 5, 5+, 5-, 5++, and so on.

Work- Value   Score
1.
2.
3.
4.
5.
6.
7.

B. Important Work Values: Now you should list seven important work values that you want in your career. These are the values wherein you have given 4 marks by ticking in the column # 4.

Work- Value   Score
1.
2.
3.
4.
5.
6.
7.

C. Next day you ought to review both the above lists to finalize your preferred sets of work values. While reviewing, you may like to shift the values from list A to B or vice versa or even from the values not included in these lists.

After identifying your desired work values, you may like to check how these relate to your current career. Here, you should remember that you cannot get everything you want from your professional life. Yet, your sincere attempt to make the best use of your work values in your future career or existing career will definitely yield rich dividends. And the above exercise is designed to provide you the right perception and the right direction to accelerate your progress.

Skills & Talents

Next step in the self- assessment process requires you to aptly appreciate your skills and talents. Broadly speaking, skills are your learned or acquired abilities and talents are your inborn or gifted abilities. It is important to understand the subtle distinction between skills and talents. However, this distinction is not absolute. Something that you classify as your talent may be a skill for another person and vice versa. In view of this, we prefer to use the term 'skills' for both skills and talents in our exercises. Moreover, from the use point of view, it is not important how you acquire a skill or talent; if you have it, it is yours to use.

People invariably enjoy doing something that they do well naturally than something they have learned to do. Skills are always acquired abilities, whereas talents may or may not be so. People usually fail to appreciate the abilities that come easily to them, whereas these natural talents can direct them to a satisfying and successful career. When your career includes more such activities, wherein you are naturally talented, you are more likely to enjoy your work and work life.

Skills are usually classified into three broad categories: Fundamental Skills, Self-Management Skills and Technical Skills. Fundamental skills are basic operational skills that are transferable from one career to another. They include thinking ability, numeric ability, communication, problem solving, managing data, processing information, and suchlike skills. Self-Management skills are the personal strengths we develop through life and work experiences. These adaptive skills are behaviours learned in families, schools, organizations, and society. They show how we carry ourselves and include attitude, personal manners, sociability, sense of responsibility, integrity, temperament, character, adaptability, etc. Technical skills are essentially the work content skills. They are usually acquired through learning and training. Generally, these are occupation-specific skills that can be used in relevant, narrow range of careers.

Skill Set

We all have many skills and talents, yet some of us may not be quite aware of our real strengths. When you analyse your skills, it helps you to identify your real strengths, which can help you to explore potentially satisfying careers. The following worksheet is designed to help you rationally analyse your skills with the aim of making a clear-cut and pertinent skills profile that can help you explore rewarding careers as well as draw on your strengths in the present career.

Profiling your Skills

I. Analysing your present Skills

To clarify your current skill set, you need to rate your skills/talents on a scale of Very Poor to Very Good as per the following directions:

> Add to the worksheet other skills/talents that you possess, but are not included in the list. (Optional step, but strongly recommended)
> You have to rate skills on a scale of E to A, i.e.,-2 to +5, where ticking × in column E means very poor= -2 and ticking × in column A means very good= +5 and column C is to mark average skills= 1.
> As per your wisdom, you have to decide your level for the specific skill and mark × with pencil in

the appropriate column adjacent to the skill description.
> You may change your judgment as many times as you like.
> This numbering system is intended to place your skills and abilities in the relative and proper perspective. The objective is to capitalize on your strengths and downplay your not so strong skills, while exploring suitable careers. However, if you wish to keep your exercise plain, you may only follow grades from A to E.

A. Fundamental and Self-management Skills

Marks >	-2	-1	1	+2	+5
Grades >	E	D	C	B	A
Skills & Talents :-	V. Poor	Poor	Average	Good	V. Good
Writing & Presenting					
Logical Thinking Skills					
Critical Thinking Skills					
Explaining Concepts Clearly					
Communicating Effectively					
Analytical Thinking					
Time Management					
Basic Computer Skills					
Web Surfing/ Internet Skills					
Identifying/Extending- Issues, Ideas, etc.					
Can Analyse and Interpret Data					
Adapt Well to Change					
Set and Achieve Targets					
Firmly Managing Barriers					
Numerical Aptitude					
Management of Inputs					... > >

Financial Planning & Management					
Being Accountable & Accommodating					
Multitasking Abilities					
Ability to bring Order Out of Chaos					
Ability to Learn New Things					
Listening Ability					
Conceptualise & Synthesize Ideas					
Initiating & Managing Change					
Positive Outlook & Conduct					
Monitoring & Appraising					
Coordinating & Persuading					
Organizing- People, Activities, Events etc.					
Problem Solving					
Managing & Motivating People					

> Next, you should make a similar worksheet for your technical or work specific skills. Here your marking system will depend on the number of items in your list so as to make total score of this worksheet equal to the preceding fundamental and self-management worksheet. For example, if your work content list has five equally important tasks, you have to give six times (30 divided by 5 assuming your worksheet A contains only 30 items) marks i.e. a scale of -12 to 30, where average corresponds to 6 marks. However, if you insist on the ease factor, you may follow only grades to profile your skills. Here, columns E and D are usually redundant.

B. Work Content Skills

Marks >	-12	-6	6	+12	+30
Grades>	E	D	C	B	A
Skills & Talents:	V. Poor	Poor	Average	Good	V. Good
...					
....					

II. Identifying your real Talents

Next, you need to enumerate your strengths and differentiate them either as skills or as talents. Remember, skills are learned abilities, whereas talents are your inborn or natural abilities. List your A and/or B grade strengths as identified in the above worksheet and check it in the second column, if you consider it as your skill, which you have been taught. Similarly check it in the third column, if that strength is your innate ability or that comes to you easily and naturally and you enjoy activities based on such strengths.

Your Strengths	Skill	Talent
1. ...	...	...
2.		
3.		
4.		
5.		
6.		
7.		
8.		

II.   Identifying Skill Deficiencies

Now you must identify the skills that you would like to improve or develop in order to take advantage of these in your preferred careers. For instance, many senior executives are not progressing in their career just due to lack of proficiency in computer skills, which is not as difficult as they think. After sensibly brainstorming over the need factor and rational motive, you are required to list your skill deficiencies, alongside your proposed action plan and target date, as illustrated in the following table.

Skills	Action Plan	Target Date
Computer Skills Expanding Issues Time Management Managing Information ...	...	...

Now you can summarize your skills profile as an outcome of the above exercises. It should also list your educational qualifications, work experience and special training you have had that can be applied in select future careers. Your skills profile provides you a handy and useful context to explore suitable careers as well as empower you to make good use of your strengths in your present career. This will also remind you about your specialties that you can use in many other vocations and social pursuits. You also recognize your weak spots and get direction to develop new skills, which are vital to advance in career. This skill profile is meant to assist you in exploring suitable careers, wherein you can excel as well as enjoy an optimal work-life balance.

Interests

Harmonizing your interests with your work is essential to ensure happiness and fulfilment in your career. Given that your career is a major part of your life, incorporating your interests in your work life is the best way to seek a fulfilling life, both professionally and personally. Your interests are the activities you enjoy. Identifying these activities, appreciating their relative importance and the ability to transfer these to your career are the crucial factors to derive perpetual satisfaction at work.

You may perhaps succeed in a career, wherein your skills and values are contributing, but not your personal interests. However, this delusory success cannot provide you happiness for long. But when you seek compatibility between your interests and your work profile by prudently matching them, you can look forward to much better outcomes in your career as well as personal life.

Apparently, identifying your interests appears a simple task, but it is not so. You may find it difficult to spell out all your principal, portable and pertinent interests precisely. It is because you are not used to thinking and talking about them, especially in the work context. So, identifying your interests and promoting them in your career calls for a proactive and assiduous approach.

The nature of activities involved in your hobbies and preferred leisure pursuits can point to your professional interests, because you like to do these activities, not that you have to do these. Similarly, your self-initiated tasks at the workplace, which are not part of your job profile, can also give clues of your interests. These ideas can give an inkling of your true and tried work interests. Besides, you should keep in mind that exploring interests is not just limited to finding the type of work you like, but it also involves examining the work environment and the social context you enjoy.

Analysing Your Interests

Though there is no clear-cut and classical approach to analyse work interests and one can do it reasonably well even by trial-and-error, it is better to analyse these in a methodical way to get a dispassionate picture. Methodically analysing your motivators can provide you necessary clues about your likes and dislikes regarding work themes, motivational drives, aptitudes, work types, work situations, workfellows, etc. in a structured manner. Let us exemplify a simple method of analysing your interests.

To simplify, shorten and personalize the exercise, first, you should recollect some of your most satisfying achievements of your work-life. You may also include a few gratifying achievements of your personal life that you often reminisce. Make a list of your top seven accomplishments from these success stories, and assign a title or number to each. Try to recognize patterns or trends emerging from these achievements that give you a sense of fulfilment. If you notice any distinctive pattern, peculiarity or aspect, that is your occupational interest. And to get further analytical insights on your work interests, you can delve into your achievements in the following manner:

1. Exploring Themes

The following table can help you explore the relative frequency of various themes appearing in your success stories. You can tabulate themes in the first column and your achievements in the subsequent columns. Now you just need to mark it against each theme in the respective achievement column if that particular theme manifests in that achievement.

Occupational Interests – Exploring Themes

Themes: Dealing with-	Achievement Title 1	Achievement Title 2	Achievement Title 7
Ideas			
People			
Things			
Data			
Social Issues			
Challenges			
...			

2. Exploring Motivational Drives

Now you need to look for the main stimulus or sense of worth you derived from these achievements. Most likely, you will find a few dominant drivers repeatedly appearing in most of these achievements. You may like to tabulate these as per the above themes table. Next, you should compare these findings with your work values assessment. In all probability, this comparison will give you clear-cut insights into your real motivational drives.

3. Exploring Aptitudes

With a view to identify relevant aptitudes that make up your work interests, make a list of skills and talents used for each achievement. Probably, you will find some abilities frequently appearing in your achievements. These are your occupational interests, especially when these are in harmony with your strengths, particularly which are identified as your talents in your skills profile.

4. Exploring Situations

In order to explore situations that can qualify as your interests, make a list of situations you often come across in your preferred achievements. You may have to tabulate situations to clearly identify the most deserving ones.

Occupational Interests – Exploring Situations

Situation	Achievement Title 1	Achievement Title 2	Achievement Title 7
Problem Solving			
Mentoring			
Convincing			
Coordinating			
Team Building			
A Challenge/ Contest			
Helping Others			
Leading Others			
Negotiating			
…			
….			

The above analysis is intended to provide you a framework to reflect on your interests and confirm whether they are consistent with other components of your self-assessment. If you observe a clear and considerable conflict between your interests and your work values, skills & talents and other apperceived attributes, it would be better to revisit your interest assessment to clear up the conflict.

We all have diverse and unique set of interests. There are innumerable factors that determine our interests. Our genetic make up, upbringing, education, social interactions, etc. influence our interests. And it is not that our interests will remain constant. As we evolve with age, our interests may change. So periodically, we need to find out whether our career and our interests are in harmony and how they can build on each other.

Understanding Your Personality

Our personality is an outward manifestation of our inner individuality. This individuality has a profound impact on our career as well as all other areas of our life. Individuals are different from each other in many fundamental ways, and that makes each individual a unique personality. But then, individuals can also be clubbed in various either/or categories, such as introvert or extrovert, feeler or thinker, imaginative or realistic, observer or judgmental, intuitive or logical, and so on. Experts believe that classifying an individual in such categories along with his personal considerations can point to his most suitable line of work.

A personality assessment looks at personal traits, behaviour, needs, and attitudes in order to typecast individuals according to their dominant personality attributes. It seeks to create a personality profile with the aim of matching it with the right careers in an attempt to harness the full potential of the individual. The premise of personality assessment in the context of career exploration exercise is that different careers fit better with different personality traits. People who choose their careers according to their personality type are more likely to be successful and satisfied with their work life. Besides, when people of the same personality type work together, they create winning combinations assuring better productivity and an encouraging work environment.

Career-oriented personality tests explore the careers that suit an individual's personality. There are many personality assessment tests available for ordinary people, such as Myers-Briggs Personality Type Indicator, Holland's Six Personality Types, etc. Without going into the merits of any particular method or even the utility and practicality of this approach that categorizes all individuals with varied traits and unique personality profiles into a few rigid categories resembling zodiac signs, we should proceed further, because our task is not to profile the personalities of young and impressionable minds, but to explore the personality traits of the mature executives, who understand their own personality styles.

By and large, 21st century executives are quite familiar with their personality traits. My experience suggests that their conditioning and experience make them the best judge to judge their personality. And suggesting them a personality profiling process is, like, a novice educatee is educating the experienced executives on their pet subject. Since experienced executives know their personality profile well, I believe they normally do not require a formal and detailed personality assessment.

But then, it may not hold good for a few disenchanted ones, who desperately need to rein in their weak spots and draw on their strengths. As a first step, they can prepare a self-report personality inventory as illustrated here below. However, they must adopt a balanced and unprejudiced approach, while appraising their traits. Otherwise, it may not provide them definitive clues due to the demonic domination of the discontent originating from their inability to cope with the stress and monotony of their profession, which perhaps make them strife ridden. And then their peremptory thoughts govern their personality and psyche, which is consistently contradicting and controlling itself, and as such, their self-report personality inventory may not serve the purpose even for remedial measures, let alone optimally harnessing the positives.

While you may not require a detailed personality assessment at this stage of your career, quickly re-acquainting yourself with the main traits of your personality can help you in exploring befitting careers. It will also help you to judiciously draw on your positive personality traits to promote your present career. In view of that, you may like to complete the following personality traits inventory wherein you have to tick it in one of these columns– Yes/ Not Sure/ No.

You have to tick all the items even if you have already assessed it in the previous exercises or you consider it trivial or irrelevant. After completing the exercise, you should again check the list for inadvertent errors and to add a tick (+) or more (+ +) to those entries, where you strongly agree or strongly disagree.

Personal Traits Inventory

Personal Traits	Yes	Not Sure	No	Personal Traits	Yes	Not Sure	No
Ambitious				Motivating			
Assertive				Noble			
Accessible				Organized			
Adaptable				Optimistic			
Affectionate				Original			
Articulate				Outgoing			
Bold				Persistent			
Calculated				Poised			
Candid				Polite			
Caring				Proactive			
Cautious				Positive			
Compassionate				Professional			
Committed				Persuasive			
Cheerful				Practical			
Competent				Precise			
Composed				Principled			
Concerned				Realistic			
Confident				Reasonable			
Cooperative				Reliable			
Considerate				Rational			
Consistent				Reserved			
Compassionate				Resolute			
Conventional				Resourceful			
Creative				Responsible			
Credulous				Responsive			
Decisive				Self-			
Disciplined				confident			
Demanding				Self-Reliant			
Devoted				Serene			
Diplomatic				Sociable			
Dynamic				Sharp			
Enterprising				Shrewd			
Emotional				Sincere			
Expressive				Sensitive			
Energetic				Smart ...>>			

Encouraging				Spirited			
Firm				Strong			
Helpful				Stubborn			
Honest				Studious			
Humble				Swift			
Humorous				Sympathetic			
Idealistic				Systematic			
Impulsive				Truthful			
Informal				Team spirit			
Independent				Tactful			
Inquisitive				Teachable			
Initiator				Thinker			
Insightful				Thoughtful			
Judicious				Trusting			
Keen				Tolerant			
Kind				Versatile			
Liberal				Vigilant			
Leading				Vocal			
Liberal				Well-			
Logical				Organized			
Mild/Modest				Warm			
Meticulous				Wise/			
				Witty			

While the above exercise is aimed at reacquainting you with your personality in general, it also accentuates positive and negative aspects of your personality and helps you appreciate how they influence your career. This will enable you to address your career issues more effectively. In addition, you can target your career search by the book.

Other Considerations

Usually the customary self-assessment exercises analyse and synthesize the above-mentioned standard reference points to create a self-profile, particularly in the context of career management. But invariably some critical factors, which can make the difference between success and failure, do not get due attention in the above standard headings. So, we need to consider some of our other self-factors in order to make our self-assessment a truly personalized and complete exercise. These factors can be personal or non-personal, external or internal, controllable or uncontrollable, enabling or limiting— but they cannot be ignored. They help us in taking well-informed decisions about our future career moves. Some examples of such other factors are:

» Our aspirations and resulting career vision
» Our present circumstances— the needs and wants of our family
» Spouse's views and life plans— her/his vision, goals, expectations
» Our willingness to relocate and our areal preferences
» Our preference for standard work timings (9-6) or flexible work hours
» Proportion of physical and mental activity we desire in our career
» Preferred size of organization— small, medium or large
» Preference for colleagues— gender and age group
» Personal health issues
» Financial health and commitments
» Aspects of our present and previous careers we liked and disliked
» Personal preference for working from home, part-time working, and suchlike factors

For many people, these other considerations can be equally, if not more, important than their skills, interests, personality and values. Many such triggers can also influence your career course, so be sure to identify them sensibly as well as prioritize them in the order of their importance to you. Your self-assessment is not complete until you assess the role of all your pertinent personal factors, particularly the serious and circumstantial issues, which can influence your career evolution as well as evaluation of new careers. This seemingly simple step just requires you to be honest and fair to identify your real concerns and commitments. Then wisely managing these factors will surely accelerate your journey on a career path that is conducive to realize your career dreams.

Summarizing your Personal Profile

Self-assessment offers two main benefits. First, the process of assessing yourself perks you up by making you sentient of your worth, which in turn helps you to pursue the right career in a self-assured manner. Second, it provides you a clear-cut and virtually complete list of your positive attributes that can help you speed up your progress. But then, a complete list is likely to overwhelm anyone, resulting in dilution of the focussed attention deserved by the principal and pertinent factors.

A summary of your self-assessment findings can help you stay poised by providing a focussed outline and a clear insight. Summarizing principal points of your personal profile can give you a real sense of purpose and a pointed direction. So, you should sum up the information gathered in the above points along these lines. You can modify your summary as and when you want, but maintain the sequence.

Self-Assessment Summary Sheet

A. Work Values— My important work values are:

...

B. Personality Factors— My main plus points are:

...

My main minus points that I need to improve are:

...

C. Other Personal Factors— My main plus points are:

...

My main unfavourable points that I need to consider are:

...

(Do leave some room for the unexpected, especially for the negative points)

D. Skills and Talents— My main strengths are:

...

Skills I would like to improve are:

...

Skills I would like to develop are:

...

E. Interests— My main interests are:

...

(Highlight the interests, which have some correlation with your identified work values, skills & talents, and other motivational drives.)

Self-assessment is a difficult and demanding process, which requires an honest introspection. And an honest and penetrating reflection on your own status can be a daunting task. But it applies to everyone. It could drive anyone over the edge. So, rather than be daunted by this challenging process, you should learn to use its complexity to your advantage to stay ahead of the competition. This you can do by clearly clarifying your most important self-factors. Bear in mind that if you are not clear about your strengths and weaknesses at this stage, you will never be able to steer the ship of your career adeptly, especially in the uncharted territories. On the other hand, making a representative summary of self-factors and appreciating it will help you further clarify your ambiguous issues, which will help you to properly prioritize your pertinent personal points. This in turn will help you to capitalize on your strong points and minimize the role of your weak points in your future work life.

On balance, it all depends on your attitude, how you take your self-exploration exercise. You can take it as something onerous and overwhelming and remain oblivious to its role in realizing your vision or you can take it as an important tool to accelerate your vision realization. Moreover, your self-assessment endeavour should not have a meaning for a day or week. Because regularly assessing yourself is an excellent way to ensure consistent progress. So to ensure a perpetual impact, one must regularly revisit it to keep it a contemporary, worthy tool for continuous self-development irrespective of the career direction one takes.

Finally, remember changing careers is not an easy option. So in the light of your self-assessment findings, reconsider if you can manage the compelling factors that induce you to seek a new career. Behaving responsibly, try to put your present career in a new perspective by identifying what is really wrong with it, especially on your part. Remember your own weak spots can trouble you even more in a new career. So first, you need to manage these barriers. Next, you should explore the possibility of unlocking your untapped potential in your present career, without sacrificing your revised vision. However, in case that seems unworkable and you are convinced that a career change is necessary for your professional progress, move on to the next chapter.

5. Explore Careers — To Discover Your True Calling

The universe of careers for the talented professionals is expanding, and this encouraging trend is gaining momentum due to growing appreciation and acceptance of the transferable skills. The technological renaissance sweeping the world of work is contributing a lot to this trend. As a result, executives are in demand not only in their chosen career, but also in many other compatible and competitive careers. While this plethora of options provides them an enviable choice, it also makes the task of choosing the most suitable career challenging and to some extent daunting. And the mature employees are aware that getting into a new and potentially bad career is easy, but getting out is difficult and very costly, considering the wastage of time, money, confidence and perhaps credibility in the process. What's more, they have to persistently preserve, protect and promote their pride and professional interests while exploring known and little-known careers.

Besides, a responsible person is not supposed to explore careers on frivolous grounds, or just to feed her/his nomadic tendencies. While seeking greener pastures, one should not forget that the grass always looks greener across the fence. Here one must bear in mind the time-tested words of Jean Nidetch, "Its choice, not chance that determines your destiny." While a good choice can take you to your dream career, a wrong choice can be your undoing. It is definitely better to proceed wisely now than to be sorry later.

Remember, your career exploration exercise can be exciting or exacting. This depends on your attitude and approach. A positive, pragmatic and proactive attitude all along will ensure a positive outcome notwithstanding whether you initiated the change or it is inflicted upon you. And a positive and purposive approach will certainly make you more employable, improve your market and provide you a clear competitive edge.

Appreciating Prerequisites

After an honest **Self-assessment,** wherein you have validated your preferred work values, skills, interests, personality, and other personal issues, now you need to explore careers that harmonize well with the essence of your self-assessment. Self-awareness is the most important prerequisite to explore a befitting career, but concentrating on it on a stand-alone basis or starting your career search therefrom will not serve the intended purpose. So, you need to visualize yourself in the context of probable careers to get the real picture. Thus, you should first see yourself in the mirror of various careers to determine your compatibility, and then explore how the compatible careers measure up to your self-assessment findings to decide which one fits the bill.

The relevant **Information** about alternative careers is imperative to achieve your goal in the career exploration process. The relevant information and data about career options help you to make a distinction between feasible and unfeasible careers. It empowers you to sort careers that can or cannot become your dream vocation. So you need to gather as much contextual and credible information as possible about potentially rewarding careers. However, one caution is in order. You must ensure that the information you use is current, because the world of work is rapidly changing. While assessing yourself, you have seen that even your profile is amenable to changes over a period. So is the case with probable professional choices where outlook and other pertinent factors may rapidly change due to changes in the various external factors like technology, economic conditions, and political changes. Therefore, you must confirm that only authentic, relevant and latest information is used to determine your best-fit and most rewarding career. In addition, remember that the career exploration is a bi-directional process wherein you may revisit previous steps if you want to clarify your choices, or change your choice(s) in the light of new information.

An **Action Plan** is the next important prerequisite in order to optimally benefit from your career exploration endeavour, which can be done in many formal and informal ways. As such, there are several methods, which can be broadly categorized into structured and personalized methods. The structured approach is highly objective, follows a pattern and usually requires guidance from a well-informed career planner. In the personalized approach, developing a career exploration strategy is an individual's responsibility. Here, you decide which resources are to be considered in the information gathering exercise and how information is to be collated. You are also responsible to devise a strategy to find pertinent facts on as many probable occupations as you deem fit. Considering your age and career stage, you may opt for any one method or a mix of both. But you must have a definite action plan, because only you are responsible for conceiving, believing and implementing a game plan to reach your dream vocation. And it pays to be in control in this exploration game, because you are investing your time, energy and finances to find a shortcut to your dream job. So, let us scan some other prerequisites to facilitate an effective and opportune exploration of alternative careers.

> A clear understanding of why you are seeking a new career
> Clarity about your career vision and the right career path to attain it
> A clear understanding of your financial situation as well as implications of a career change on your financial health
> Reasonable, whole-hearted support of family and friends (expecting and relying on an unconditional support is inherently unreasonable)
> A clear understanding of what type of careers you should avoid keeping in mind your profile and previous experiences

> A conviction in your vision, an uncluttered vision orientation, and a keen desire to make it
> Willingness to try your best. Acknowledging the fact that your today will give birth to your tomorrow
> A resolve not to get discouraged midway on trivial issues. Ensuring a conducive and supportive environment all along.
> Ability to understand the difference between inferential information and de-facto information
> Wisdom to purge the urge to jump to conclusions on unreliable facts and facilitating decisions after proper research
> Following the art of asking yourself the "what ifs", particularly before taking any decision
> A well-informed and understanding mentor (You may consider an intelligent friend or spouse. The two/three of you can make a great team to review career options prudently.)
> Resolve to act rationally rather than emotionally, react pensively rather than instinctively, and follow the planned career course rather than straying.

Changing Employer vs. Changing Career Direction

At this stage, one should clearly understand the difference between changing employers and changing career fields. A quest for changing your organization, but not your career domain implies that you are seeking a change in the employer. And when one is satisfied with the work content and work environment in the present organization, but enjoys less than perfect rapport with the boss, one may rather wish to change only the boss within the same organization. Often it entails a minor change in the work life and it is practically possible in many organizations, particularly the large ones. And as such it may not be termed as a career change depending on the nature and extent of change.

On the other hand, changing career direction implies that one is seeking an opening in other occupations. There is a big difference between changing employer and making a career transition. Changing career field allows you to redesign your career path in a new direction. So, it typically entails some changes in other areas of your life as well. Since this change could be a life changing transition, it demands a firm conviction in the reasons to change career lanes. So this major transition requires detailed working to minimize the risks and maximize the coveted rewards. In fact, changing career direction calls for a total commitment in order to succeed in the unknown territory.

These days, career seekers change jobs, employers, and careers on a regular basis. In most occupations, this trend is gaining momentum crazily with the advent of new technologies and globalization of the workforce. But some people chose their first career after adequate career planning, and they do not get easily tempted by the short term trends or materialistic gains. They really know why and when to consider a career change. They also know when it is time to change jobs and when it is time to change careers. But then, not all may be accustomed to taking the right and requisite initiatives in their career.

The old saying, "the grass is greener in other fields" is very relevant in the context of career change. New careers are not always what we think they will be. One should not presuppose that a big change would be a better change. So, one should first explore the possibility of a change within the organization, next within the known career domain and lastly in the exciting, but unknown universe of the alternative careers. Then again, actually, it depends a lot on why one is seeking a change. In fact, the compelling grounds for seeking a change point to the type of change one should seek.

The career exploration process delivers better results when we initially expand our options a bit casually, then narrow down our choices systematically, and ultimately choose the best one wisely. Here we intend to discuss the career search process with reference to the literal career change, i.e., assuming you are open to change the career direction. So, this process entails exploration of all careers in order to screen out the viable ones. If you are contemplating just a change in the employer or perhaps only the settings or the boss, you may suitably simplify and shorten your career exploration exercise to suit your purpose.

Expanding your career choices

This step is not just about finding careers that conforms to the prescription ordered by your self-assessment. Rather it is more about discovering as many potentially satisfying careers as possible. The objective is to stretch the scope of your prospective careers. Here, your career expectations and willingness to retrain will play a major role in identifying suitable occupations. You are not supposed to go by your coloured whims and fancies to unnecessarily preclude any potentially rewarding career. At this point, you need to break away from the shackles of preset notions, including your professional vision. And to be open to new ideas and new careers, you need to ensure that your right or wrong perceptions and mental blocks do not impulsively block any worthwhile opening.

First, make a tentative list of alternative careers that come to your mind. Next, look up other reliable sources to seek latest information on other credible careers. The occupational outlook handbook from the bureau of labor statistics is a good primary source of career information. It is designed to provide valuable assistance to individuals making decisions about their future work lives. The Career Guide to Industries, which presents occupational information from an industry perspective, is also an excellent resource for career changers. You can also explore information on job opportunities related to your interests that you may not have thought of with a personalized tool on the Bureau of Labor Statistics site.

While examining various alternative careers, you might have viewed some occupations more approvingly than others. In this process, your subconscious mind — with many relevant inputs from your self assessment and other career relevant insights — was at work. Therefore, you are likely to find your most suitable calling within these favourably rated careers. Now, after sensibly scanning the universe of your probable careers, you are simply required to shortlist some careers for further scrutiny in a systematic manner to identify your dream career.

Narrowing your career choices

Unlike the previous step where you could carelessly luxuriate in the extra choices, possibly paying not much attention to the all-important self-factors, here you need to follow a careful and cautious approach instead of a somewhat casual approach. At this juncture, you need to identify viable career options on the basis of a well-coordinated screening process that accords adequate importance to harmonizing your self-profile and career attributes to ensure a satisfying outcome. Accordingly, you are now required to narrow down your list based on the established parameters in a rational and systematic way. In view of this, you have to screen your preferred careers considering your self-assessment summary to weed out superfluous entries. Here is a simple way to sift through your list of probable careers by matching them with your important motivating factors, as established by the self-assessment process.

Directions:

1. In the first column, note down all careers short-listed while expanding your career choices in the previous step.

2. Subsequent columns are meant to show how a particular career relates to your self-assessment findings— representing work values, skills & talents, interests, personality and other personal factors respectively.

3. On the basis of your summarized personal profile as prepared in the previous chapter, you need to appraise each career with reference to each motivational factor on a scale of +2 to -2 where +2 = very favourable, +1= favourable, 0= neutral, -1= negative, -2= very negative.

4. Last column represents total score for a particular career.

5. Sort the careers in ascending order based on the total scores.

Career Selection Worksheet
(Scale: +2 = very favourable, +1= favourable, 0= neutral, -1= negative, -2= very negative)

Career Options	Work Values	Skills & Talents	Interests	Person-ality	Other Factors	Total
Public Relations						
Financial Planner						
Consultant-Relationships						
Business Support Services						
Marriage Counsellor						
Media Surveyor						
Content Writer						
Customer Services						
Games/Toys Creator						
Kids Products Promoter						
Upbringing Consultant						
News Correspondent						
Admn. Officer						
Insurance Consultant						
Children's Party Planner						
Human Resources Pro						
Market Research						
Career Planner						
Dance/Music Trainer						
Wedding Planner						
Resume Writer						
Motivational Speaker						
Data Gatherer						
Workshop Presenter						

Prioritizing Top Three Careers

The above career selection worksheet enables you to simply cream off cream of the crop careers, which are consistent with your self-profile. It provides a framework to evaluate each career with reference to important work values, skills, interests, personality and other personal factors as well as objectively rank the careers according to their scores. Careers with better scores are your obvious picks for further detailed scrutiny.

However, this simple and otherwise well-balanced scoring system has a limitation; it does not give graded weightage or veto power to any factor. Such a rational and robotic method may not always be compatible with the human nature, which is composed of innumerable variables often contradicting and contrasting each other. So, in order to give adequate emphasis to your sensible perceptions, you should pick a few, preferably three to five careers, which rank high in your career selection worksheet. It is not necessary that you pick the top three or five careers. These careers ought to give you a feeling that they will harmonize well with your long-term career vision. In fact, your penchant for some activities that invariably manifests as your preference for the related careers can offer you dependable clues to your most suitable calling. Your subjective view is intended to balance a somewhat overly objective evaluation in the previous step. Besides, it ensures that your subconscious is also contributing through your sixth sense in deciding the top picks, which you should list in order of preference for further detailed analysis.

Provisional Career Choice 1, that is to say, Public Relations

Provisional Career Choice 2, … …… … ……

Provisional Career Choice 3. … …… … ……

Finalizing the Best Career

At this stage, you are clear about your viable choices; you also know what you want to do and what level you should aim. In all probability, you have many ideas about your future career, but some of these may be vague, because you have not formally tested the ideas or even methodically brainstormed over these. Besides, the chances are that you are experiencing inquisitive exhaustion, especially if you have done the above exercises very swiftly or very casually. You are particularly vulnerable if you are changing career for the first time because your mind may be grappling with known and unknown, real and false deterrents.

However, changing careers is not easy for anyone. Usually, it is taxing and testing to finalize a future career. The process is likely to overwhelm anyone in view of the consequences of such a major decision. So, the following steps are meant to psych you up, so that you can remain serene and objective while concluding your career search. These clear-cut exercises will help you to connect with your dream career in a very simple and structured way.

The purpose of the action plan suggested below is to focus your thinking on a select set of parameters to evaluate your select careers. The objective is to facilitate an objective evaluation in a subjective manner to ensure the most favourable outcome. Here are the validating steps to finalize your coveted career from your list of best picks.

Appraising Career Openings

1. This step involves appreciating various opportunities in your selected career domain. Here again, you are supposed to follow the process followed while short-listing careers. In fact, these choices are a subset of your chosen career, and you are required to pick the most suitable one. To illustrate, we assume that a career in public relations is your first tentative choice. Now, you are supposed to identify the best lines of work in the public relations and allied fields. You can easily make your handpicked list of alternatives by first expanding the list, then narrowing it, and finally finalizing it. First, you need to list all probable careers in this field, as depicted here below. Now you can strike off the careers you dislike from the list. Next, you need to visualize yourself in the remaining career options and brainstorm at least for two minutes on each alternative and highlight the favoured ones. You can use number of ticks (i.e., + or ++ or +++) to put your relative preferences in perspective.

Exploring Preferred Career Domain

Openings in Public Relations	Comments
Public Relations Executive	++
Media Coordinator	+
Corporate Trainer	?
Educational Consultant	+++
Business Area Representative	*
Corporate Spokesperson	+
Institutions Spokesperson	
Political Party Spokesperson	
Business Campaigner	
Social Activist	
Freelance Public Relations Services	
Communications Coach	
Public Address System in Charge	
Services Demonstrator	
Media Strategist	
Product Promoter	
Career Counsellor	
Charities Fund Raiser	
Reception In-charge	
Information Officer	
Celebrity's Spokesperson	
Advertising and Promotions Manager	
Admission Coordinator	
Area Representative	
Meetings and Convention Planner	
Consumer Coordinator	

2. After prospecting various career titles in the previous step, now you need to examine different work settings related to your chosen

career titles. You can select your preferred work environment from the following sample list of some work settings.

Exploring Preferred Work Environment

• Industry	• Health Centre
• Institution	• Recreation Centre
• Social Organization	• Book Club
• Your Home/Your Office	• Political Organization
• Small Business	• Schools/Universities
• Services Provider	• Tourism Organization
• Advertising Agency	• Charitable Organization
• Media House	• Malls & Multiplex
• Hospitality Sector	• Sports Complex
• Fashion House	• Social Club

3. Next you ought to brainstorm over your definition of success. You should mull over how you define success and what does it mean to you: wealth, satisfaction, authority, contentment, status, giving, sharing, etc. After clarifying it, examine how your elements of success relate to your newfound career titles.

4. Now you need to verify whether any additional skills are required to enter and advance in this career. Study the personal qualities of those who are successful in this career.

5. Understand the work environment for your tentative career — indoors, outdoors, working alone or with others, and the like. Comprehend what it means to you.

6. Study the outlook of your new career and guesstimate future demand vs. supply situation. Do you anticipate any threats or opportunities in the near future from external factors like technological developments, economic situations, etc.?

7. Get your process of selecting your newly defined professional identity validated from a trusted friend, preferably a mentor who can also guide you during the difficult times in the career change phase. However, make sure that she/he is willing to spend time

and energy in order to really contribute in the career selection process.

8. The final step in the decision-making process is to envision a mental picture of yourself and your new career over the next few years i.e. two years, five years, and ten years. Also, visualize whether this goes well with your long-term career vision and how you will feel about it at the end of your work life.

After completing the above exercises, the next step is to conclude the advantages and disadvantages of your newly found career option(s). You should keep in mind that you are likely to find some negative points in all the careers. Your objective should be to maximize the favourable factors and minimize the impact of adverse factors in your future career. In this analysis, you are supposed to consider your professional factors as well as your personal issues. To sum up the analysis, you should tabulate all the positive and negative points for ready reference.

Next, you need to repeat the above exercises for the remaining provisionally selected careers. This will enable you to prudently compare your tentative options so as to finalize your perfect career with conviction. This simple analysis will help you to confidently decide the most suitable career in a rational way. In case your chosen career turns out to be in the self-employment mode, you may skip the next two chapters, which deal with changing jobs.

Taking time to explore viable careers and appreciating them is an energizing exercise for any person seeking a career change. Irrespective of the career direction you take, it will help you realize your career vision quickly. Even if you decide to take a U-turn, that is, a second thought about the career change, it will still help you, both professionally and personally.

6. Tools & Techniques — To Get the Job You Want

When it comes to seizing opportunities, our evolution, conditioning and education could not make most of us any better than the predatory dinosaurs. We often manifest the same level of conviction on our arbitrary and muddled way of thinking as dinosaurs used to have on their instincts while preying. But then, it is not right to blame our education or our evolutionary conditioning, because the real culprit seems to be our self-induced, self-indulgent way of looking at life that gives rise to our senseless, headstrong attitude, which in turn prevents us from following a disciplined and structured approach to get what we truly want. Predictably, more often than not, our success depends on chance rather than our choice.

Besides, we spend donkey's years on learning several things except the career management. Most of us show reluctance to invest a few hours to learn the art and science of seizing opportunities in general and the job search in particular. Though we spend a lot of time in flirting with the idea of a great job or perhaps excitedly seeking a good job, we rarely do it in an ordered, well thought-out and professional manner. Nearly all of us know the importance of a good job in our life, but a very few take up their job search methodically. Most of us are used to take this either as a secondary activity or as something that can be handled in an arbitrary manner. In fact, for most people job search means sporadically sending résumés to employers, like indiscriminate firing from a scattergun. And their dismal success rate— in getting interview calls or job offers from the worthy employers — is a testimony to their imprudence.

But then again, most of our education acquaints us with knowledge on several subjects, but hardly any ideas about how to effectively put that to work while seeking work. Perhaps, our education system is lacking, when it comes to following a pragmatic approach to our career issues. Some cosmetic exercises even with the genuine interest are quite inadequate to make a real difference, especially in the case of the deserving class, i.e., lesser mortals. Therefore, we typically continue with our haphazard approach until a cul-de-sac compels us to come out of our cocooned comfort and initiate on our own a proactive and organized approach towards our career issues.

And then, we realize that it is not the most competent individuals, who get the best jobs; rather, it is those who are most competent at finding the right job. In other words, it is not that the best candidates get the best jobs. But the candidates, who can convince the employers that they are the best candidates, get the best jobs. It is not that merely their education and luck help them convince the employers. In fact, they are lucky to get the jobs they want because their job seeking tactics are better than their peers. They are well prepared to seize the opportunities. Their tools are ready and their techniques are in place. While the knowledge is important to get a good job, but knowing the process of job search and exploiting it optimally makes all the difference between a mere eligibility for a job and getting the job. So, re-acquainting yourself with the job search skills is really important to seek your dream job.

Updating Your Job Search Skills

Finding a suitable job is not a reactive or passive process just involving actions prompted by the external stimuli; rather it should involve proactive, positive and poised search strategies, aptly supported by the effective tips, tools and techniques. Besides, if you do not adhere to a well thought-out process, your job search may possibly test your conviction in your career vision. On the other hand, if you follow a practical and persistent approach, certainly you will get the job you really want.

Most candidates' own view of the job search process is too narrow and shallow, often constrained by their conditioning. Some candidates just seek a quick and convenient way out to end the uncertainty in their career, especially when they are disenchanted with their present work situation. They do not adhere to a proper job search process and opt for a quick-fix approach. Consequently, they often take impetuous and irrational decision to choose another inapt employment without realizing that they cannot afford to play games with their career. On the other hand, some people are over-literate in their career domain. What it implies is that they are over-knowledgeable about their career sphere, which tempts them to overindulge and thus overreact in their own career quest. As a result, they get overwhelmed while seeking a change in an arbitrary and know-all manner and consequently give up their chase. And some rigid ones surrender midway owing to their heady cocktail of arbitrariness and unreceptive attitude towards new careers.

But then again, many candidates rationally take full advantage of the job search skills and realize their professional aspirations. Therefore, it is imperative for every job-seeking person to work on updating the requisite job search skills before initiating the job search. Here are some other benefits you can expect from an organized job search process.

✓ It improves your prospects of getting the right job that blends well with your long-term career vision.
✓ It gives you conviction in your campaign and confidence in your potential to succeed.
✓ It provides you a 360° view of the process and thus boost your self-confidence, which in turn helps you aptly manage change-anxiety.
✓ It enables you to carry out an effective and efficient job search, thus saving time, energy and money.
✓ It helps you de-focus from the past setbacks and re-focus on the exciting new openings.
✓ It gives you some control over the highly unpredictable process of job search.

✓ It helps you present yourself and your credentials in a much better way that makes a positive impression on your interviewer.
✓ It makes you conscious of your weak spots and thus enabling you to minimize their likely impact on the prospective jobs. It also makes you amply aware of the positive and negative aspects of a job prior to choosing it.
✓ Your systematic working impresses the prospective employers, who view you positively, which gives you a competitive edge over other job seekers.
✓ It provides you an objective that continually motivates you to act, and act rationally. It also gives an achievement orientation to your campaign that subconsciously strengthens your desire to succeed.
✓ Finally, and importantly, it makes you more employable for your envisioned job.

In this chapter, we will discuss the tools and techniques to facilitate a self-directed, responsible job search. While devising and implementing your job search strategy, these tools and techniques will help you to optimally integrate the various pro-active as well as passive parts of the job search to ensure better outcomes. These tools and techniques will not only accelerate your job search, but will also create winning opportunities in line with your aspirations.

Tools for Effective Job Search

In order to optimally benefit from your career change, you need to bring into play a few handy and practical job search tools as an integral part of your game plan. Though, your most important job tools are your skills, but your skills will not get you a good job, unless you convince your prospective employers about your skills and talents. The job search tools help you do just that. These tools will not only make your search more effective, but will also enable you to manage your resources more efficiently. Here are some valuable job-seeking tools.

A Right Résumé

We all know that a résumé is the first and foremost tool in the job search process. We also know that it is meant for recruiters. Yet, we often fail to view it from the recruiter's perspective. And if we view it from the employer's viewpoint, we tend to go overboard to please them and in the process, we often cross the acceptable boundary of a true and trustable account. We also err, when it comes to the presentation part and often go off the rails on the relevance and brevity fronts. However, here mature executives fare much better since they understand that there is always scope for improvement.

Your résumé should be an honest confession of your accomplishments and academic credentials. It must be a clear, convincing, concise and precise document. With a view to get an upper hand over the competition, it should emphasize your skills, experience and strong points in such a way that clearly establishes that your credentials are well matched for the position. I personally feel that it should also show a glimpse of your certain negative or deficient aspects, as it will help you not only at the time of selection, but also afterwards if you get the job. Otherwise, also there is no point in betraying the prospective employers, because only you have to face the music sooner or later. Besides, no one expects you to be perfect, and any sensible recruiter will appreciate your candour and admission of deficiencies. Moreover, we all know that everyone has some limitations and even God does not claim to be perfect.

Standard guidelines for résumé writing may not fully serve your purpose, because candidates have different résumé needs, which again vary depending on their age and career stage. Therefore, writing an effective résumé requires you to first understand your résumé needs inline with your career change vision, so that you can accordingly create the right résumé framework. Your résumé framework should be simple and well-structured, so as to facilitate flexibility. Since a standard résumé should not be used for all job applications, a flexible framework will enable you to easily customize it to conform to the requirements of different positions. This flexibility will allow you to highlight your specific skills and fortes suitable to a specific job. And that you can do by researching the organization and the post you are applying for. This will make selectors especially interested in you, and this initial edge will set you apart from the competition. Here we again outline some important pointers to write a winning résumé.

- Keep it simple, factual, precise and practical. Use active verbs and bullet points to make sure that every word counts. Add an aptly designed cover letter to generate interest.
- Depict applicable job skills and work experience prominently. Stress on the relevant skills and achievements, which relate well to the post. Do not exaggerate; you will be wasting more time, even if you make it to the interview based on that. Also, avoid irrelevant information.
- Modify your résumé according to the job applied for, so as to clearly demonstrate your value and suitability for the job. Within the limits of a true and fair account, strive to orientate it to the pertinent profession and the post applied. Focus it on the needs of the potential employer rather than your needs.
- Never write anything negative about present or past employers. Never reveal employer's proprietary information.
- Write a few bullet points to highlight your major, relevant and eye-catching achievements. Do not be modest here and look forward to explain your achievements in an interview.
- Give good references, preferably from the associated fields. Avoid insouciant persons.
- Make use of your professional vision as well as formatting skills to give it a professional and personalized look. Remember that your positive attitude towards the application for the job sends the first positive signal.
- It is not always easy to spot your own errors. So, get the résumé critically reviewed from a trusted and informed friend or spouse, before you send it.

One Minute Spoken Résumé

Your success in the selection process depends firstly on your first impression. Remember that you never get a second chance to change that first impression. A first impression can evoke three responses— positive, negative or confusing; a positive first impression takes you to the next level in a positive light, a negative impression usually implies that you are out of the game, and a confusing impression may perhaps give you another chance to prove your mettle. Your first impression depends on you as well as on the sensitivity of the selector or interviewer's antenna. While you cannot do much about the second factor, you can surely firm up your part. And a short résumé can definitely help you do that.

Your short and snappy verbal résumé is a great tool to promote your job search campaign. Potential employers and your network can help you get that dream job only if they are aware of your strengths and your career vision. You need to design a self-promotion strategy and start talking to the relevant people, who can either provide job leads or bolster your campaign in other ways. Simply put, you have to market yourself. And you must remember the old saying, "You only get one chance to make a good first impression." You should also keep in mind that our brains are wired to form impressions automatically and very quickly. So, you just get 10-15 seconds to create the interest of other person to ensure that he attentively gives ear to your talk. Then if the situation permits, you may well justify your suitability for the prospective job in the next 30-45 seconds. You should be prepared for further discussion if the other person is willing and able. Therefore, you should use this tool only when you are ready with all other tools for the job search. A standard verbal résumé typically attempts to address the following questions.

➢ Why you are seeking a new employment?
➢ What skills and expertise you can offer?
➢ How your work history and professional strengths relate to the job in question?
➢ How this association can be a win-win situation for you and the prospective employer?
➢ What makes you special and different from other candidates?
➢ Why this new employment is important to realize your long-term career vision? And how?

Changeover Portfolio

Your career change portfolio is a handy and multipurpose tool wherein you organize all information relating to your career change and job search. It not only helps you throughout the job search process, but also proves invaluable in the job interview that is the most important and difficult part of the process wherein you have to stand on your own. In the interview, you cannot seek any external help except for your portfolio, which can help you there in many ways.

In your résumé, verbal résumé and other tools you need to be concise, but here you can luxuriate in details and incorporate detailed as well as short versions. To arrange your information and data methodically, you can use a good quality folder with dividers and display sections to organize your portfolio. There cannot be standard guidelines to organize the contents in a portfolio, as it varies from case to case depending on the individual's personal profile. Yet, just to elucidate the concept, here we give some basic tips on what a portfolio should contain.

1. Résumé and Cover letter

2. Personal Information:
   - Career Vision statement
   - Qualifications and Certificates
   - Skills and other assessments
   - Experience records
   - Workshops and conferences records
   - Membership of professional bodies
   - Other relevant personal information

3. Testimonials:
   - Character references
   - Positive appraisals
   - Articles about your calibre and potential
   - Pictures of awards, prizes, medals, etc.
   - Commendation letters
   - Appreciation letters/ articles

4. Work history:

- Documentation of key skills
- Professional accomplishments
- Management examples
- Writing examples
- Published work
- Other relevant information

5. Information about industry and organization:
    - Articles and news about industry
    - Other statistical data and information about industry
    - Articles and news about employer
    - Other data and statistical information about employer
    - Your research findings about career field and employer

6. Your preparatory documents:
    - Synopsis of your self-assessment exercise
    - Synopsis of your career exploration exercise
    - Synopsis of other exploratory and research initiatives

7. Questions you would like to ask from recruiters/ mentor.

Portfolio Advantages

A carefully planned portfolio not only differentiates you from other candidates, but also provides many direct and indirect advantages. Here are some advantages of your job search portfolio.

> Confirms your sincerity
> Illustrates your groundwork
> Develops self-confidence
> Reminds you about your goals
> Demonstrates that you are well-organized
> Proves you are disciplined and methodical

> Substantiates your résumé
> Keeps you motivated and stimulated
> Presents evidence of your achievements
> Simplify as well as accelerate your job search process.
> Surely yet subtly campaigns for you

Most importantly, it provides you a context and framework in the interview to highlight your skills, abilities and accomplishments in a professional manner.

List of Positive References

It is important to select your references very carefully, because they not only give the right initial impression, but can also make or break your case at the confirmation stage. You need not opt for high profile persons as references, if they do not know you well. You should prefer persons from the same or associated fields, if they know you and your career profile. They are more likely to give a detailed feedback about your potential as well as give positive signals. Some basic tips on choosing the right references and coordinating with them are given below.

➤ Choose references who know you for quite some time.
➤ Take their permission before giving their names as references.
➤ Never select any controversial or insouciant person as reference. Avoid persons from competitors group and political persons. If you have a career mentor, s/he can be the best reference.
➤ Update your references not only about specific jobs, but also inform them about your career vision that prompts you to seek a better job. However, create as little intrusion as possible.
➤ If possible, involve them in your job search process as they may give you a favourable lead.
➤ Prepare them with personalized and handy feedback that they can use to endorse your candidature.

Working Folder

A working folder is a good idea for employed executives to keep all the essential items required in the pursuit of a new job at one place. You have the option to keep all these things in the portfolio as well, but it can unnecessarily clutter the portfolio, which is primarily for demonstrating your worth, and not for routine working purposes. This folder should contain all preparative papers, other relevant papers, stationary and other job search supplies. Your working folder, or a functional subset of it, should be handy to facilitate convenient reference at all times. You may not like to engage in job-seeking activities during your work hours, but you cannot afford to dodge communications from potential employers in this age of instant communication channels. Here, a subset of your working folder can prove a very handy tool. Your working folder can provide you pertinent information at your fingertips, wherever you may be, if you are carrying the relevant part of it. Your productivity in the job search process increases considerably by systematically maintaining a working folder along with subfolders for specific purposes.

Personal Support System

A personal support system is important for all career changers. But it becomes crucial for the working people, especially when they are seeking an alternative employment discreetly and do not wish to disclose their career plans at their workplace until they tender their resignation.

First, you have to determine your needs and accordingly engage a suitable support system. It can help you in several job seeking activities such as, research of careers, gathering information, generating job leads, analyzing trends, manning your desk, and the like. Your personal support system can also take care of your interview dress, private computer, internet connection, web activities, stationary, and other necessary supplies. If you do not require or cannot afford private support services, your spouse, or a family member, or a friend can fit the bill, while you are at work. You simply need to coach them what is expected from them. Then you can expect them to play their part according to the script. And if you wish to handle some important matters exclusively yourself, you should candidly spell out the boundary; besides, clearly inform them how to handle the communication channels on both the sides of that boundary.

Worksheets

Finally, it is advisable to have some self-priming and self-monitoring tools to carry out your job search in an efficient and result oriented manner. The following worksheets can help you to make the best use of your time and energy in this endeavour.

i. Job search programme

Your job search programme should consist of all the necessary steps, which you have to pursue to get your preferred job. You are required to list all the planned activities with the expected completion date. Next, you need to divide these activities in a clear-cut weekly to-do-list. Here is a simple table depicting weekly job search programme.

Job Search Programme for the week   11.11.11 to 18.11.11

S.N.	Particulars	Target Date	Status
	...		
	...		
	....		

ii. Job leads worksheet

Creating job leads for a career changer is not the same, as it is for a career entrant. Here, job experience and accompanying goodwill plays a big role that can really help you in your campaign. It is especially true for the key executives, who do not enjoy the same degree of freedom and flexibility as ordinary people do. While it is important to create job leads, it is more important to keep track of these to optimally tap the important job leads. So, you should design your simple and practical worksheets to monitor activities of generating leads, tracking leads, and managing these to get a competitive edge in your job search process.

iii. Job evaluation worksheet

It is meant to document your assessment of all the important aspects of a prospective job. This tool works best in tandem with the technique of researching a job, discussed in the next part of this chapter. Preferably, it should be made separately for each job. Here is a typical format of job evaluation worksheet.

Job Evaluation Worksheet

Job Reference No.	Application Stage	Pre-interview Stage	Post-interview Stage
Compatibility with your Career Vision			
Compatibility with your Self-assessment			
Compatibility of Work Culture			
Future Outlook and Growth Prospects			
Other Advantageous Factors			
Other Adverse Factors			

Techniques to Get the Job You Want

The route to your dream job is not easy. But a rough and tough route cannot distract you from your goal, provided you equip yourself with the potent tools and powerful techniques to sail through the rough weather. Here are some techniques that can help you in your search for a dream job in a practical, self-directed and responsible manner. These techniques will show you an effective and result-oriented way to get your coveted job. So, you can look forward to convert a 'wild-goose chase' to a 'will-get chase'.

Job Targeting

Job seekers, who carry out a targeted job search, enjoy the highest success rate in finding a gratifying job. On the other hand, when job seekers opt for a 'flexible' or 'open-to-any-job' approach, they unnecessarily waste their time and resources. While trying to cover too much territory, they lose focus and often end up again in a dissatisfying job.

Choosing clear-cut and credible job targets is an efficient way of winning the job quest, particularly for busy people. This is truer for the working executives seeking alternative employment. Job targeting entails identifying certain industries, locations, organizations, and specific titles in the selected organizations. It is imperative to evaluate the demand vs. supply situation sensibly at every stage in your targeting exercise. Your chances of getting the right job improve considerably, when you direct your efforts to the right targets.

After analytically assessing yourself and exploring your career options, you have the requisite wisdom to select the suitable and viable targets, where your employability quotient is greater. And the following important and obvious pointers will help you to target your job search more precisely to further enhance your prospects.

»   Target the industries and work environments that harmonize well with your long-term career vision.
»   Select the locations as per your personal preferences, but confirm whether your preferred locations promise suitable jobs and favourable long-term outlook.
»   Target the organizations, where success rate of getting your desired job is higher. You can consider the size and work culture of the organization as well to target perceptively.
»   Target organizations with proven track record of growth. Or else you should be confident of prospective employers' future growth plans. You will make better progress in your career if your employer organization grows.

» Select your job title targets as per your personal profile. Focus on the titles that go well with other elements of your job targeting exercise.

» While targeting suitable jobs, you may like to consider some other factors relevant to your job search— such as selecting targets, where your network or accomplishments can play a significant role. Identify your specific factors to focus your search.

You will get more clarity on your job targeting exercise when you conduct a comparative analysis of your present job vs. preferred job, which is a part of the last job search technique discussed later in this chapter.

Discreet Job Search

It is wise to carry out the job search discreetly, particularly when one is employed. While a discreet job search may be somewhat difficult and likely to take more time as well, yet it is the advisable way to job hunting. An employed person is expected to perform well in the current job. Job security may have lost relevance in today's world, but employers still expect loyalty from the employees.

When you are employed, you are in a privileged situation as far as your employability quotient and other personal factors are concerned. So, you need to consider your job search as an important and indispensable part-time activity that has to be done without putting your present job at risk. Maintaining an optimum balance between the two is the key to enhance your prospects. It seems simple, but careful execution can be quite demanding depending on your situation. So, you have to think through your situation and make a checklist to keep your job quest discreet to the desirable extent.

Even while leaving your employer, adhere to the same policy and depart humbly. It may not be a 'good-bye' forever; it may be a 'see-you-later'. No one knows. So, it is advisable to be modest if you are going to a better job. It is peculiarly odd to brag about your new job, as that serves no useful purpose but can impact your career negatively. And without a doubt, it is better to quit as discreetly as possible, while leaving under coercion.

Researching the Job

One true-and-tried technique to get ahead of competition is shrewdly researching the job under consideration. Rightly researching the job at an early stage can provide you many insights in time. This will help you to focus only on the worthwhile positions, instead of dissipating your energy on many otiose job leads. It primarily consists of researching the organization, the post and the employer. Researching a job is no rocket science; you can do it easily with the help of right information sources.

In order to intelligently investigate the organization, aptly analyse the post and wisely look at the employer, you have to first look for pertinent information in the public domain such as, organization's website, balance sheet, brochures, catalogues, media reviews, and news archives. Next, you can seek informational interviews with the past and present employees to get wise to the insider information. These sources will adequately equip you to mull over the following important aspects.

i. The Organization
- History of the organization
- Field of activity, Organization's vision, mission and emphasis on social responsibility
- Size of the organization, number of employees, turnover, and ranking in industry/field
- Infrastructure/Capital employed/Size of Balance Sheet/ Profit and Profitability
- Locations— head office, branches and future expansion plans
- Future plans and outlook of the organization— whether in growth mode or not
- Performance track-record on stand-alone basis and how it compares with competitors
- Public perception of the organization, and suchlike factors

ii. The Post
- Position and number of vacancies
- Nature of job, expected skills and abilities, work content
- Remuneration, non-pecuniary benefits, retirement terms and other work values
- Principal duties and how these match with your interests and personality traits
- Direct or indirect relation of duties to social service, your hobbies and your personal vision
- Area of posting, transfer policy, any contract or service bond
- Working hours, working conditions, workfellows' attributes
- Growth prospects, incentive policies
- Whether job profile harmonize well with your professional vision
- Matching other factors that originate from your career change vision statement

iii The Employer
Researching the employers is not the same as researching the organization. While researching the organization, you are more concerned with the hard part of the institution, whereas researching the employer is all about evaluating the soft aspects of the institution. It is like evaluating the software while buying a computer i.e. hardware. To succeed in your endeavour, researching the employer is as important as the right software is to the optimum functioning of a computer. And it requires you to carefully examine the management style, work culture, collegial harmony, seniors' sensitivity to juniors, juniors' respect for seniors, other behavioural aspects and suchlike factors.

However, people usually treat this important component of the job evaluation process rather casually and callously. They have a tendency to jump to convenient conclusions about an employer before joining. They realize the negative aspects only after joining when it is too late for any course correction. And then, they find no recourse, except to look for another job. Even then, they defend their casual approach by re-arguing how one can assess soft aspects without actually experiencing them first hand on the job and pass the buck to their bad luck, the favourite whipping boy.

But then, it is not that difficult to read the signs before joining, if you use your common sense and gut feeling well. How you are treated in your interactions with the employer points to how you will be treated after joining. Another important pointer is the body language and attitude of other employees. If they appear cheerful and lively, you can rate the soft aspects of the employer and staff positively. You should also give ears to the market grapevine as well, but judiciously. Besides, you should seek inside information and first hand account from the horse's mouth. When all is said and done, you have to uncommonly use your common sense to make sense of the feedback, especially from previous employees because they are likely to be biased.

Understanding the Selection Process

Though finding out the entire selection criteria may not be possible in most cases, even understanding a bit of it can give you a competitive edge, and hence improve your success rate. While a few organizations are quite forthcoming about their selection criteria, others are at the other end of the spectrum, i.e., completely tight-lipped on their evaluation methodologies. But most employers prefer to follow a middle-of-the-road approach, which offer you many inputs and cues to follow a more focussed approach. So, wherever possible, you must avail the opportunity to understand the selection process and prepare yourself in light of that to hit the mark easily. Here are some clear advantages of acquainting with the selection process.

✓ When you know the selection criteria as well as your status, you can prejudge your chances of succeeding. And that enables you to aim only at the attainable openings to save time, efforts and money.
✓ When you know the desirable qualities and their weightage in the selection process, you can prime yourself accordingly in a more focussed way so as to draw on your strengths and work on your weak spots.

✓ When you know what is expected from prospective candidates, you can easily cope with the anxiety and nervous feelings associated with a changeover, particularly the interview part.
✓ You do not become a victim of unrealistic expectations.
✓ Knowing the likely interview agenda can help you predict probable questions and prepare accordingly for the occasion.

Monitoring your Web Presence

Though getting a job depends a lot on your skills, it is important to present yourself rightly, not only through traditional modes such as resume, references etc, but also on the all-pervading web. The ubiquitous internet has redefined the rules of communication and recruitment function is no exception. Recruiters have long browsed the web to seek and sift potential employees, but now they are also browsing blogs, networking sites, and suchlike channels to gain insights into candidates' credentials. Earlier recruiters used to frown on social networking sites like, facebook, myspace, twitter, orkut, etc, but nowadays they scour these as a part of their selection evaluation process. A latest survey by career media company Vault shows that 44 % of employers are logging in to social networking sites to examine the profiles of job-seekers.

The web can be a vehicle to display your candidacy to the prospective employers. It can also subtly campaign for you as well as support your credentials. So, you should devise a strategy to leverage on this important medium. You can create, promote and manage a website, discussion forum, or a blog on your area of expertise to supplement your web presence. You should frequently monitor your web presence and periodically refresh it in line with your current changeover objectives. Remember, your sharp and gripping online footprint works as a professional relationship builder in addition to improving your professional appearance.

Remember that we all have an online identity, whether we know it or not. So, ignoring it may possibly affect your prospects negatively. It depends on you whether you control it or it controls your prospects. However, you should keep in mind that using the social media merely to get a job can be counterproductive.

Comparative Analysis of Preferred Job Vs. New Job

As our identity is defined by what we do, we have to clearly understand and carefully consider how we feel about that identity in our career, especially while opting for a new career. We also need to consider whether we like the look of the career path ahead of us or not in addition to whether the way ahead lives up to the ways of the world. While materialistic considerations are important, eventually we need to prefer quality-over-quantity route. Here, we must tap our inner instincts to finalize our career roadmap.

By and large, executives are not just governed by the materialistic mind-set in their life, and that clearly manifests in their career endeavours. Yet in a status conscious society, it is easy to get tempted and accept a job merely because of visible status perks and pay packet. And it is not fair to expect candidates to be completely immune from such human vulnerabilities. So, with an eye to obviate such odds, you should develop a simple, yet well-structured framework representing as well as clarifying what you really want in your next job. A well-structured framework takes into account all the decided elements of your preferred job.

This preparatory technique seeks to re-acquaint you with what you should seek in your new job. Here, you need to tabulate all the relevant and important factors in the first column of your comparative analysis table, as illustrated hereunder. Second column shows how these factors fare in respect of your present job. The next two columns represent your range of expectations by specifying what you want and what you will accept in a new job. And the last column is meant to facilitate an easy and rational scrutiny of your new job offer. In order to objectively evaluate every new job offer, you can make copies of your evaluation table, which will help you decide robotically in the initial stages.

Appraising New Job Offer

Particulars	Present Job	New Job- What You Want	New Job- What You will Accept	Job Offer# 2
Financial Rewards				
Designation				
Hierarchy/Reporting to				
Location				
Working Schedule				
Impact on the Family				
Contribution to the society				
Synergy with Career Vision				
Job Profile Synopsis				
Work Settings Synopsis				
...				

Given that only you clearly and comprehensively know your personal needs and wants, you can always add some personal tips, tools, and techniques to make your personal job search strategy more effective. You can also tap the experiences of successful career changers, particularly from your field, to augment your career-change wherewithal. However, it is not prudent to blindly follow anyone's footsteps because your profile, circumstances and personal needs can only determine what is best for you. So, learn from achievers' tips, tools, and techniques and selectively use them to give a fillip to your job search campaign.

Your tools and techniques along with appropriate job search methods will empower you to get your envisioned job on your terms. Remember that the right tools, right techniques, and right search methods are the vital components of your job search strategy. And how you capitalize on the interplay of these components will determine your prospects. In the next chapter, we will examine the job search methods.

7. Job Search— Ways to Your Dream Job

You are looking for your dream job and some employers are on the lookout for suitable candidates for that kind of jobs. Perhaps some employers are desperately soliciting people like you to fill the important positions. But the question is how to find these openings, especially when most of such vacancies are not adequately advertised. Often good job openings are hidden, because employers usually resort to rough-and-ready and rushed measures to fill the important positions. Invariably, good positions are vital from the employers' viewpoint; hence, they hanker after eligible and readily available candidates to fill these important positions urgently. And they often enjoy a ready supply of smart and swift candidates for such important openings through various direct and indirect avenues. That is why they prefer to bypass the traditional channels of recruitment whenever they can make use of more efficient and more dependable methods of recruitment. In view of that, it is very important to understand and appreciate various job search methods so as to formulate a winning job search strategy. Moreover, the dynamics of the job market makes it a must.

Remember, your job search is your responsibility. You must bear in mind that you are looking for a good break not just another job. And understanding the role and relevance of various job search methods in your profession as well as your specific case is the key to effectively and efficiently carry out your job search campaign. Your restricted view of the job seeking ways may not provide the requisite momentum needed to take your campaign to the logical conclusion. The biggest downside of focussing solely on your favourite job search method is being short-sighted about hidden job prospects that can provide shortcuts to your career vision. Preoccupation with any particular job seeking way can be as detrimental to your career growth as a rudderless approach to seeking a new job. In view of that, you have to evaluate all the contemporary methods and then tap only relevant and result-oriented job search methods to seek a convenient shortcut to your coveted job. This will substantially increase your prospects.

However, first of all, you need to psych yourself up considering that your job search can be a wearisome process, which may test your conviction in your potential on the way to that special job. And you need to harden your heart too to ward off some enticing temptations on the way.

Besides, a sense of urgency and unrelenting urge to avail any route is not the positive way to realize your career vision. Rash and reckless decisions should have no place in your game plan. You have to be patient and selective to execute your campaign effectively. You can surely progress to your dream job by prudently identifying and diligently pursuing suitable job search avenues. It may sound like a laughably simple tactic. Yes, it is, yet it works. It is a result-oriented tactic since this aspect of your campaign is totally under your control. It can make your job search as effective as possible, while preserving your self confidence in this weary process. That is why knowing about various job seeking ways is one of the most important keys to be a winner in this game. And the exceptional success of many of your colleagues is a testimony to this belief. So, before finalizing your job search game plan, you should first choose the job search methods you will use to make contact with the prospective employers. Here we look at some of the most effective job search methods, particularly suitable for career changers.

Networking

The process of purposive interaction with people who can potentially provide useful job leads is known as networking in the career jargon. Career Networking entails talking to people about your career vision that compels you to seek a specific kind of job to achieve your career goals. This effective method of job search requires you to selectively circulate information about your career plans and gather information about potential opportunities through interactions with resourceful people.

However, career networking is not the same as social networking. Career networking revolves around making professional connections that can help you promote mutual professional interests. Though social networking is intended for social purposes, nowadays it is increasingly becoming a validating tool in the hiring process. Many employers have developed a fancy to scour the web, particularly the social networking sites like Myspace, Facebook, Orkut, LinkedIn, Twitter and the like to check the credentials of prospective employees as well as present employees.

The importance of networking for the professionals seeking a career change cannot be overemphasized. While it is useful for any job seeker, it is particularly suitable for the career changers seeking senior positions. Experts unanimously agree that networking is a good source of great jobs for professionals as it has the greatest success rate amongst all job search methods.

Your job search network should primarily consist of professionals who can guide you and also volunteer a few referrals to increase your net of people. Your relatives and friends can also be a part of your network to speed up your job search, but well-known professionals from the chosen career field are more effective. They can offer you an insider's view and provide you worthy leads to the hidden jobs. Spreading the word among the domain professionals is the best way to break into the hidden job market. If a person you speak to cannot help you directly, she or he may perhaps put it to somebody who may possibly provide the job leads you are seeking.

Employers prefer this recruitment method because it is the most efficient, cost effective, and reliable way to appoint trustworthy people. Employers are happy to employ a recommended person, as they need not go through the time-consuming hiring process to engage a worthy candidate.

Moreover, they still prefer the traditional 'who-you-know' approach to fill the important vacancies despite all the talk of open recruitment policies. That is why networking with the professionals in your chosen career field can put you on the right track, which can quickly take you to your coveted job. Even though I am a proponent of a level playing field and transparent systems, particularly, when it comes to the career opportunities, I recommend employers to opt for the recommended candidates to fill the important positions considering the benefits of this avenue to both the employers and employees. Here are some winning tips to use networking in your job search campaign.

✓ Develop your network in conventional, as well as novel ways. Broaden your network by getting referrals from your resourceful contacts and the persons in the loop.
✓ Do not tell everyone that you are actively seeking a change. Selectively inform only relevant and influential persons. Remember, professionals in the related field or organizations can be the most suitable referrals.
✓ Briefly introduce. Be specific, yet give them a good idea of the type of job you are seeking and also explain why. Clarify what you expect from them.
✓ Be ready with the pertinent information, when meeting new contacts. Without asking, you should prove that you are worth endorsing.
✓ Your information and requirements should be clear and specific to make it easier for your contacts to remember.
✓ Ask for advice and gather as much relevant information as you can.
✓ Do not take too much time of your links. Yet keep them informed about the developments.
✓ Keep in mind that good interpersonal skills are crucial to make it via networking.
✓ You should be willing to say and substantiate what makes you stand out above other job seekers
✓ Do not consider dodging as downers. And do not get disheartened. One cannot expect encouraging response from everyone in today's 'time saturated world.' Take avoidance in your stride and move on.

✓ You should be willing to reciprocate in a genuine way.
    Spend some time helping others.
✓ Keep your connections alive. Regularly update them.
    Liberally show gratitude and write thanks letters to leave
    a positive impression.

Direct Employer Contact

It is also a proactive job search method. To a casual observer, it gives the impression of a rough, uninvited move, trespassing on the employers privileges, but in fact, it is one of the most effective and practical method of job search, particularly for an experienced person seeking a career change in the area of her/his expertise. It differs from other traditional methods wherein opening move is usually from the employers' side. Therefore, many people are not at ease with this self-initiated method owing to their deep-rooted perception that it is an employer's prerogative to seek employees and not vice-versa. Moreover, they feel uninvitedly contacting the employer tantamount to debasing yourself. And it gives the impression of a desperate measure that usually does not go well with the prospective employers. However, it is usually not true, especially in the case of progressive employers, who routinely welcome candidates through their websites. Besides, a carefully crafted initiative can address the false or factual concerns of such adversaries.

Further, the success of this avenue largely depends on how you take the first step. Remember the purpose of your first communication is to arouse the interest of the recruiter, so that you get an invitation for a detailed personal meeting. And if you get an encouraging response, you need to plan a good follow-up strategy, which is equally important to capitalize on the success of the first move. So, you need a well thought-out plan and a sensible strategy to succeed through this method of job exploration.

This method is for you, if you are good at direct marketing. Contacting employers to seek a job is a kind of direct marketing, where you have to sell your skills. While marketing your credentials, you have to be conscious of the requirements of your potential customer, i.e., the employer. So, you have to keep this in mind while formulating an appropriate strategy to contact potential employers to prospect a suitable job. Your strategy should be flexible enough so that you can customize it to accommodate the specific needs of each potential employer in addition to your personal preferences and present situation. That is why you could do well with a mix of communication channels as well as tactics to touch base with the prospective employers.

Any person who is willing to take a sensible initiative and has the ability to get on the right side of the prospective employers can expect a good success rate from this method. However, this approach is not suitable for the introvert people, who are not comfortable to get in touch with the future employers without a reference. But then, even such people who dislike directly approaching employers can adopt this method along with other job search methods, whereby they can first establish a formal link, and then they can directly contact employers with reference to that. Here are some simple steps that can help you to use this method tactically.

- First, you need to decide the category of employers you want to contact and then decide the communication channels you intend to use to contact them. Your self-assessment summary and the relevant information on the prospective employers can help you decide these two important factors.
- Make a list of the potential employers, who are likely to be on the lookout for candidates with a personal profile like yours.
- Carry out a preliminary research on the organizations, career field and probable jobs before contacting the organization. In the light of this information, scrutinize the listed employers with a view to shortlist i.e. delete, modify or add to the list.
- Consider contacting the concerned senior most executive personally or make a call to seek a face-to-face interview with the relevant executives. Alternatively, you may send

your résumé first to the concerned executive and then
follow up by a call for a face-to-face meeting.

- Do not give the impression that you are desperately
  seeking a job. Do not start by inquiring about vacancies.
  Indirectly explore the possibility. Be prepared to explain
  how you can give your best to the organization in a specific
  kind of job and how this will help you to realise your career
  goals.

- Comply with the directions, like a request for the résumé or
  prescribed application form, and continue your direct
  follow-up thereafter.

- Take negative responses as a normal part of the process. Do
  not take anything personally and strive to keep the link
  alive.

- If you get a chance to present your case, use your job search
  tools optimally. Be ready to explain your professional
  vision. If this is a preliminary meeting, your verbal résumé
  is the key to getting an invitation for a detailed interview.

- Your changeover portfolio can help you to make it to the
  top in the main interview. Use it judiciously to capture or
  divert employer's attention to your unique selling points.

- To enhance your prospects, you need to keep the ball in
  your court. So, shrewdly try to take the responsibility of the
  follow-up at the end of interview/meeting.

- You can explore the suitability of your skill sets for a
  particular organization by researching the growth plans
  and human resources needs of that organization. In view of
  that, you can even try to convince the employer to create a
  position that corresponds to your skill sets as well as your
  career vision.

- Be generous in sending the thank-you letters on every
  possible occasion.

While a follow-up is important in all job search methods, it
is crucial to succeed in this method. So, you should keep a
systematic record of all follow-up actions. Maintaining a direct
contact log will not only enable you to keep track of your progress,
but it will also help you to maintain your credibility with the
prospective employers. Here is a typical format to record your
progress. You can change it as per your needs.

Status Report– Direct Employer Contact

Details	Employer ABC	Employer PQR	Employer XYZ
Position Contact Person Employer Address Phone Mobile Fax E-mail Research Synopsis Contact Details:	.... Mr Getit ABC Inc ... ...@...... ... ... Ist call – résumé asked/sent In-person meeting on 11.11.11		
Status Viability Suitability	Next meeting on 17.11.11 Average Very Good		

Jobs Advertisements

Another common and established source for all kinds of employment opportunities is job advertisements in the media. Although ubiquitous job ads provide a level playing field to all job seekers, yet they are more popular amongst career beginners and not so discerning job seekers. However, most job seekers pursue this method to some extent, because it provides definite and handy leads to the vacancies at all levels. However, it is not a great source of opportunities for job changers seeking true career gratification because the majority of good jobs are not widely advertised. And in view of the fact that it is very convenient for everyone to peruse the advertised positions than the unadvertised ones, the competition is invariably tough here. Besides here, one has to compete with many deserving, as well as socially deserving contenders.

It may not be an ideal method of job search for the purposive professionals, but it suits media and mediators well as it serves their commercial interests. With the propagation of newer communication channels, the job advertising is not just limited to the print media. Though, newer channels are giving a serious competition to the long-established print media and some alternatives to the users, but their business models are also based on the profitability considerations akin to the print media. While it seems they are serving the employees and employers needs, but in fact most of them are more concerned about their shareholders and perhaps the advertisers, i.e., employers who are regarded as a revered revenue stream. And most communication channels are running over each other to make hay at the cost of whey, while crème de la crème looks away. When all is said and done, one cannot afford to ignore the underlying importance of this mainstream method in any job seeking initiative. It is only a question of how and how much one avails of this indispensable avenue to further one's prospects. And that will be dictated by one's age, career stage and grounds to change.

What's more, vacancies publicized in the newspapers, magazines, internet, and other electronic and print media provides useful service to the job seekers by keeping them abreast of the latest employment trends in the various segments of the economy. Besides, this full-fledged industry provides direct and indirect employment to millions. And unquestionably, it is a very good source of information on the ordinary vacancies, especially for the career entrants. Even aspiring or enterprising professionals can make good use of the job ads to generate rewarding job leads, which may not have been publicized, but can be pursued in view of the initial information gathered from these ads. Here are some basic tips.

- Search for useful job ads only in the credible and relevant sources. You should be clear about the medium, as well as the channels in that medium that suits your profile. If you have a specific profession in mind, look for professional publications or vacancies for that category published in the reputed sources.
- Keep details of all such vacancies that look like viable options. Research the organizations. Gather as much information as possible. Then analyze the vacancies in detail before responding.
- Be wary of the ads that appear too good. Diligently investigate about the organization before responding to such ads.
- Apply within stipulated time to avoid rejection because of delay. However, in case of delay, you can call the hiring authority to seek permission. Sometimes, this works in the candidates favour.
- Your cover letter should meet all the requirements specified in the ad. Remember, your application is carrying your first impression to the recruiter, who knows nothing about you.
- Tailor your résumé in the light of each selected advertisement so as to appropriately highlight the desired strengths.
- You need not be excessively cautious about the eligibility criteria concerning all the qualifications, skills and other requirements specified in the ad. These should not deter you if you think the job is a good fit for you. However, shrewdly clarify the correct status as well as how you intend to make up the deficiency.
- Personalize your response if practical. If specific names are not accessible, address to the decision-making position. If workable, send a copy to the decision maker in addition to the person named in the advertisement.
- Examine whether networking and/or direct employer contact can be gainfully used along with this method.

Private Recruiters

Private recruiters or placement agencies offer an efficient medium to seek a job in line with the job aspirant's needs and desires. They are the experts in the field, adept in searching a suitable employee for a particular job. Private recruiters are supposed to be good at analysing employee and employer in the best possible way. They are basically professional agents working as an informed link between employers and job seekers. Moreover, most good recruiters know the job scene very well. Their services range from just categorized mailing services to the other end of spectrum where they offer complete career solutions, including career planning guidance. The specialized recruiters are more appropriate for the career changers with special needs.

The trend to fill important positions through the private recruiters, who follow fair practices, is gaining momentum. Usually, they get the assignments to hunt suitable candidates from the employers, who are their clients. More and more employers are opting for their services for the preliminary functions of the recruitment process. However, most employers prefer to keep the final interview and selection evaluation process with the in-house executives. The following reasons persuade employers to outsource many activities of the recruitment process to the outside recruiters.

- By outsourcing pre-employment activities, employers save time, money, and other resources. They can concentrate on their core activities, as private recruiters can conform to the need of speed, cost optimization, and other hiring objectives.
- They get worthy candidates screened and short-listed by an independent source. They prefer to deal with candidates endorsed by a known source.
- They can keep the recruitment process relatively discreet from the competitors, external and internal employees.

- Employers can avail special services offered by the recruiters, which employers may not be in a position to do on their own, e.g., contacting talented employees working with the competitors and influencing them to sign up for the important positions.
- Private recruiters can provide important feedback on the industry trends as well as competitors strategies in the human resources area. These vital inputs can help employers in formulating their growth strategies and human resources planning.

In addition to the above points, most employers find it easy to outsource the initial selection part to an agency that fulfils their criteria and is in a position to meet their current requirements. Employers enjoy this obliging choice, thanks to the recruiters of all types and sizes. For the reason that makes the employers and the recruiters a team with an unreasonable upper hand, a job seeker has to be extra cautious in choosing a private recruiter. Besides, some big recruiters may prove to be fussy and fastidious recruiters, because they like to maintain their success rate and reputation through dubious and devious means. Higher success rate shown by them is a fallacy as they take only selected candidates and getting good jobs for the cream of the crop is not a big deal. On the other hand, some recruiters may attempt to lure you in a job, which does not match well with your profile and career vision, just to earn their fees. But then, many good recruiters work in a professional manner. They believe in a fair play and follow fair practices.

This source is very important for career changers, because these professionals are well-equipped to appreciate their career concerns and aspirations. Sincere private recruiters understand and appreciate job seeker's career goals. And then, they suitably guide job seekers, who can look forward to gratifying job leads. Here are some rudimentary tips to consider while selecting a private recruiter.

- Try to find an established agency catering to exclusively your preferred career field. For career changers, specialized recruiters providing services in their specific field are better than all-purpose recruiters. If possible, choose a private recruiter active in your geographical area.
- Keep in mind that you are not just seeking mailing services. Opt for recruiters who understand the job change process well, both from employers as well as employees' perspectives.
- Avoid those recruiters, who are just interested to fill the vacancies and are oblivious to the job appropriateness concerns.
- Before finalizing your contract, investigate the credentials of the recruiter. Understand conditions of the contract before signing it.
- Check how much it will cost you. Some recruiters charge from both the employees and employers. The revenue models of recruiters vary significantly; examine it to assess their suitability in your game plan.
- Clarify the scope of work and try to understand their methodology. Keep in mind that they have a divided loyalty between the employers and the candidates. Not many recruiters maintain an optimum balance and provide a fair play to a job seeker.
- Some agencies also provide career planning guidance. They usually charge more, yet they can be a better option, especially for a confused career changer.
- Discuss your strengths and interests as well as your weak points. Candidly discuss with them how these can be exploited to make your résumé more impressive. Find out whether you need to tailor your résumé for some special positions.
- Convey your preferences of locations, employers and positions. Agree on the judicious forwarding of your résumé and not mass mailing of your candidature. Discuss your requirements of an inconspicuous job search.
- Take recruiter's opinion on your choice of references. Also, explore whether and how the agreed references can be convincingly used to back up and promote your campaign.

* Make only selective use of your job search tools. Do not reveal all your exclusive tools, especially in the initial stages. Remember agencies may just provide some leads and not jobs.

Other Methods of Job Search

Some other methods of job search are employment services provided by states/ social societies/ professional associations, job fairs, job competitions, electronic bulletin boards, resume referral systems and suchlike services. More often than not, these methods do not suit experienced executives looking for a new job, because they usually have a very low success rate. And a high failure rate usually triggers frustration, which can adversely affect momentum of your job search. Further, they can lead to unnecessary publicity of your job seeking efforts. Therefore, it is advisable to stick to the time-tested and more suitable methods discussed above, instead of wasting your resources on these secondary methods.

But then, there is one method in this category, which is very convenient and offer almost sure selection. Sometimes executives seeking a career change join their self-employed spouses expecting it to be a blessing in disguise that often turns out to be a curse in camouflage. Remember, some make it big via this lucky break; others risk not only their professional identity, but relationships as well. So, here again you need to move carefully.

After having a clear understanding of various avenues to seek a job, now you are in a position to plan your job search more prudently. However, you should not rush. Rather think about the most effective avenues to target your coveted job. Then incorporate the suitable ones in your action plan and systematically follow it to get the job you want. This way you can create a better job search plan based on the efficacy of various methods. The following table outlines an estimate of the popularity and the efficacy rankings of various job search methods. This may perhaps help you to make an efficient plan to accelerate your job search.

A Comparison of Job Search Methods

Job Search Methods	Popularity %	Efficacy %
Networking/ Personal Contacts	32	41
Direct Employer Contact	35	28
Advertisements	72	14
Private Recruiters/Placement Agencies	25	29
Others Methods	28	8

Remember that the point of perspective is not 'which is the best method?' but which suits you the most. Efficacy rates of various job search methods vary considerably depending on various factors, like type of position, line of work, geographic location, and other factors influencing the demand-supply situation. You need to decide whether you would like to use a particular method of job search or a combination of methods to carry out your job search effectively and efficiently. However, it makes sense to include two or more avenues of job search in your plan to achieve better results. Often, prudently selected methods build on each other and provide greater momentum to your campaign. Remember that keeping yourself updated and well-informed on the new hiring trends will help you choose the winning methods. And whatever avenues are chosen, the key point is to make sure that your job search strategy is in line with the contemporary trends of the dynamic jobs market. This will help you to find some method in the madness of a rapidly evolving world of employment.

When you choose the right methods, you can look forward to positive outcomes, but sometimes outcomes may not be what you wished-for. So, be flexible. Periodically step back to gauge the effectiveness of various avenues by assessing exertion to outcome ratio. While a few methods may not work for you, others may require some fine-tuning as per your needs. This will help you modify your action plan in line with your experiences. Keep in mind that job seeker's ability to modify their job search strategies according to the market dynamics is the key to success. So, be critical of yourself and explore how you can improve your search. And periodically, reflect, refine, and redirect your campaign if you need to.

The job search is an art as well as a science. Remember, an efficient job search is your responsibility. And it requires persistent efforts in a systematic manner to get the job you want and deserve, and not just another job. Reckless job changes can be counterproductive to your long-term career plans. You ought to make sure that you are heading towards your career vision, and not just running away from your present job. Preferably, your new job should take you to a higher learning curve as well as meet your motives that motivate you to seek a new job. You owe it to yourself and those around you to make the best use of your talent to get a satisfying and rewarding job that takes you towards your envisioned career vision.

8. Employing Yourself — Planning your Business

More and more people are realizing that the 21st century will be the century of entrepreneurship like the last century is known for creating fulltime jobs. Already, it is evident that entrepreneurs, and not the state, will play a dominant role in creating career opportunities in future. And in this era of information explosion, the knowledge entrepreneurs will obviously dominate the domain of work. Appreciating these trends, nowadays most enterprising and venturous people consider it better to look for business opportunities rather than seeking jobs. However, some diffident and risk averse people are reluctant to accept this on-going transformation of the world of work, wherein the role of alternative modes of work is expanding at the expense of full time jobs, where the relative growth rate is continually falling and this trend is expected to continue in the foreseeable future. And the self-employment mode accounts for the lion's share in the newer, growing work opportunities. Yet, full-time employees have many and divergent opinions about the self-employment route. Most of them are expectantly keeping an eye on these developments to make sense of the upcoming trends so as to recognize future opportunities and challenges.

Traditionally, executives are reluctant to experiment or explore the entrepreneurship, thus robbing themselves of an exciting opportunity to use their multifaceted abilities. Some executives turn to entrepreneurship by default rather than design. However, it is gradually changing and nowadays executives are increasingly showing the guts to try beyond the tried and tested careers. The misconception that entrepreneurship is only meant for aggressive and adventurous people is slowly and surely fading away.

Executives yearning for freedom at the workplace quest for a business activity, whereby they wish to draw on their latent talent and thus control their destiny. Also, the ambitious and enterprising individuals, who are tired of the humdrum atmosphere of the 9 to 5 workplace, eagerly seek the bliss in self-employment. Besides, with the advent of the internet era most executives are keenly looking at the independent ways to make the most of their potential to serve the humanity at large. For executives seeking flexibility of time and workplace, self-entrepreneurship is the best way to pursue a gratifying career. Moreover, the emergence of knowledge economy and the potential to make it big is firing up the dreams of gifted individuals, and also influencing the risk-averse executives' mindset.

But then, appreciating the trends and becoming a part of the trend are two different things, with vastly different consequences. All executives are supposed to keep tabs on the relevant trends. But only eligible and willing executives should explore self-employment, preferably in their area of expertise. However, their business universe should not be limited by their expertise; go-getting executives having requisite talents can explore any area showing a genuine demand pressure from the society. They can consider any business, where the products or services are in demand. They should not be deterred by many myths and misconceptions concerning entrepreneurship. With a view to address all the potential start-ups, we intend to interchangeably use the terms self-employment, business, entrepreneurship, vocation, venture and firm.

Myths about Entrepreneurship

While some professionals are taking the plunge into entrepreneurship to realize their career dreams, many others are still sceptical about it. They are not comfortable even with the thought of exploring it as an alternative career. It is not that they are averse to the idea of becoming their own boss and enjoy unrestricted access to wealth and fame. And they are definitely not allergic to the term business. In fact, many myths surrounding the terms business or self-employment or entrepreneurship, restrain them. My experience suggests that most professionals do not consider self-employment as a career option owing to several myths associated with it. Even some professionals from the field of business management are susceptible to some of these common myths. So, it would be better if we first examine and pre-empt these myths so as to create a receptive mood. Here are some important myths associated with the entrepreneurship.

Risk Myth: It is a common but false perception that success in business necessarily entails taking huge financial risks. Successful enterprisers are not gamblers, nor are they speculators. They are by and large risk-avers people like most of us. But they understand their risks well and strive to minimize them. Successful entrepreneurs have confidence in their ability to manage risks. When they take risks, these are calculated risks based on their astute assessment of the favourable risk-reward ratio in order to maximize their gains. Moreover, there are many businesses, which involve negligible financial stake and thus negligible financial risks.

Capital Myth: Many people believe that entrepreneurship requires huge capital, and that is the most important ingredient to create a business. But then, history confirms that the majority of successful entrepreneurs started their business with the modest capital, mostly from their personal resources. Moreover, average start-up capital is not too much and is definitely within the reach of most professionals. Then again, there are many occupations, which are not at the mercy of money. The booming knowledge-economy has further marginalized the role of money in creating businesses. However, raising capital is usually not as easy for an entrant as it is for an established entrepreneur.

Age Myth: The word entrepreneur conjures up the memories of a few young people who achieved super success at a very young age. These rare cases give further credence to the widely held notion that entrepreneurship is more appropriate for young people. But it is not true, as confirmed by many studies. A recent study by Vanderbilt University confirms that more and more middle aged and aged people are taking up entrepreneurship. This trend is likely to gain further momentum. Besides, several surveys confirm that middle age is the average

age when qualified people embarked on their first business venture.

Furthermore, we must remember that ordinary individuals' lifecycle follows a typical pattern, youth looks ahead, middle age looks tired and old age looks back. On the other hand, achievers are never tired; they always look ahead. They can achieve success in business at any age.

Idea Myth: It is a popular notion that in order to succeed in business, you have to have an innovative idea or a high-tech invention. But the fact is that exceptional execution is more important than exceptional idea to make it in the business. Breakthrough ideas can deliver value only if executed well. Then again, the majority of people have achieved success in business by meticulously carrying out average ideas.

Paraphernalia Myth: Many people believe that adequate paraphernalia is a prerequisite to start a business. Though it is important to grow in many businesses, it is not a necessity for many start-ups. Then there are many vocations, especially knowledge-based and creative occupations, wherein it is usually not required. Some people also consider that a place to conduct business as well as the formation of a company or firm is necessary to start a business. It is not true for many promising vocations particularly in the initial stages. However, adequate paraphernalia, though not essential, is an asset in any business venture.

Luck Myth: Many people believe that success in the entrepreneurship depends more on the luck factor than on the entrepreneurial abilities. They also believe that external circumstances play a greater role in the success of a business than controllable factors. It is true that success in business depends on a host of variables, including external factors. But usually most of these variables play as per our abilities and as such can be appropriately managed. It is a proven fact that successful enterprisers are adept at capitalizing on opportunities and they invariably make it, because of their abilities and, not due to their luck. On the other hand, people who fail to spot or cash in on the opportunities, try to take shelter in the luck factor.

Apprehensions

In addition to the above-mentioned general myths, there can be many other case specific false fears, mistaken notions, and erroneous assumptions associated with businesses that deter many people. Professionals may be adept at dealing with such trepidations of other people, but they are often not as good, when it comes to their own misplaced apprehensions relating to the entrepreneurship. They easily fall prey to many misconceived notions about it. For instance, fear of unknown is a very common and potent worry that comes in the way of the entrepreneurial aspirations of many professionals. However, when such professionals explore their principal drivers that prompt them to take up the self-employment route, they can see through their short-sightedness, the light at the end of tunnel that, inter alia, sheds light on their apprehensions and place them in the right perspective.

Entrepreneurship is often perceived as a high-risk high-reward kind of proposition. It may not be necessarily true. But one ought to understand and respect the risky tag, not necessarily accept it. The risk is usually venture dependent, and one can start many ventures without taking much risk. However, no one can guarantee success in this line of work. Only you can enhance your prospects of success by exploring suitable vocations, planning well and executing plans wisely. In fact, entrepreneurship can be very satisfying both professionally and financially, if undertaken in a well thought out and planned manner.

But then again, without reasonable reasoning, one should not be at the other end of the spectrum by taking shelter in the oft-repeated saying, "self help is the best help, self analysis is the best analysis and self-employment is the best employment", as it has contextual relevance. Self-employment cannot be the best employment for every one. Or it may be suitable near or in retirement, but not at the current ascending stage of the career curve. While it can be fun, fulfilling and financially rewarding for some, it can be fraught with failure for others. So you must be very clear why you want it.

Do you really want it?

While contemplating self-employment, it is important to look at the reasons why you want to take the plunge in the private enterprise. What are your leading drivers that encourage you to explore the entrepreneurial route? Whether these originate from within, i.e. internal reasons like an intense desire to be independent, earn more, or excel professionally, etc. or these stem from external conditions, such as dissatisfaction in current career, career stagnation, health condition, or a compelling need for flexibility? How will these factors operate and affect you if you continue in your present career? How will they affect you if you do not succeed in the proposed venture? Thinking about these questions will help you to rationally explore the tempting domain of entrepreneurship, where one cannot afford to be a diehard optimistic or an unfair sceptic. One has to espouse a realistic approach, while assessing entrepreneur's qualities in order to wisely explore this domain.

Entrepreneurs' Qualities

It is not just that professionals are well aware of general skills and abilities required for entrepreneurship, they even possess most of these. In spite of that, it might not be suitable for every professional. Many professionals are risk-averse by nature and conditioning, because our education system is geared towards employability factor rather than creating employers to create employment. Therefore, professionals develop a predilection for secure and steady life style. Entrepreneurship may not be suitable for such professionals. And it is certainly not for the faint-hearted. However, these generalized arguments may not apply equally to all the vocations undertaken in the entrepreneurship mode, as well as to all the professionals. Even though most professionals know the general qualities that determine a person's suitability for entrepreneurship, these qualities deserve a cursory mention.

+ Vision to work for self
+ Keen desire to achieve & earn
+ Perseverance
+ Willingness to take initiative

+   A strong urge to explore
+   Realistic planning skills
+   Risk taking potential
+   Self-control/ Amenability
+   Soft skills/ People-friendly nature
+   Domain expertise
+   Desire to make it
+   Competitiveness
+   Confidence/ Commitment
+   Capacity for hard work
+   Ability to manage stress
+   Determination & Discipline
+   Good Health
+   Capacity to withstand uncertainty
+   Ability to manage people
+   Analytical mind

You may further explore this option only if you are at ease with most of the above qualities. You also need to have a firm conviction in your entrepreneurial idea before you invest your time and money on it. You should reconfirm whether your entrepreneurial idea is a realistic one and entails a favourable risk-reward ratio. Analysing the following questions will help you determine whether you can make it in the private enterprise.

• What motivates me to opt for self-employment?
• Does my personal profile go well with entrepreneurship?
• Am I clear about my niche for entrepreneurship?
• Am I ready to take moderate risks and cope with some uncertainties?
• Am I ready to serve multi-roles within my small organization?
• Does my Idea really draw on my skills and abilities?
• Do I understand the market for my product and/or service?
• Do I possess planning, organizing & decision making skills?
• Do I have the support of my family & friends in this venture?
• Am I willing to make the sacrifices necessary to get my venture going?
• Can I endure emotional and financial setbacks during downturns?

The dependable assessment of self-needs and how these can be addressed by the contemporary opportunities is central to the enterprise decision. So, if you are not comfortable with any of the above questions, you need to first deal with it, or devise a strategy to skirt the issue in point, before you rush headlong. Then you can analyse all the factors in favour of and against your decision to go in for the entrepreneurship. To do this in a rough and ready yet objective manner, take a sheet of paper and start writing pros on one side of the paper and cons on the other side. Continue this brainstorming exercise for some days in an impassive way. Please make sure that this practice does not overwhelm you. The real purpose of this exercise is not making a perfect list of pros & cons; rather, the objective and the real worth is in the practice of exploring all justifications for and against your decision to undertake this route. This seemingly simple exercise will not only give you clear insights about your idea, but will also prevent many detrimental steps.

Exploring your Forte

Some occupations are more conducive to the self-employment mode than the rest. Exploring a suitable self-employment occupation requires you to assess the synergy of your skills with the occupation as well as the long-term potential of the occupation under consideration. Professionals normally take the self-employment route to make the best use of their skills and as such, usually their expertise is the deciding factor in their career choice. Yet, it is desirable to accord equal importance to the personal interests and to the long-term outlook of the career line so as to ensure a rewarding and fulfilling work life. However, one should scan all available options, before committing to the preferred one. It will not just give you a bird's eye view of the plethora of opportunities, but in this process you may possibly stumble upon an occupation that has certain synergies with your chosen career and combining these may provide additional revenue streams just with a fraction of accompanying expenses, thereby multiplying your profits.

You will find many self-employment opportunities. The key is to understand what fulfils your professional vision, and what does not harmonize with it. In order to bring to fruition your career vision, you simply have to target your niche of the market, so as to take the best advantage of your skills and interests. There are many specialized subsets in any business line, and you ought to select that subset of your selected business wherein your skills are in demand, outlook is encouraging and most importantly, that fascinates you.

Assessing Viability

It is very important to take the challenge of career change in a well thought-out and systematic manner, as we know that career change is one of the most important decisions of our life, especially opting for entrepreneurship, because it involves higher stakes. Many times, professionals boldly and blindly enter entrepreneurship. Your success in the entrepreneurship depends largely on whether you undertake it in an intelligent way or an inept way.

It is pertinent to touch on your marketing strategy at this stage to enable you to mull over your chosen self-employment option in a rational and realistic manner. It is important, because customers will be your real bosses here. You may be confident of your value for money proposition, but your customers may think differently. Moreover, you are either not accustomed to customers, or at the most just have indirect and ringside view of this faceless tribe. So, with a view to pragmatically assess the viability of this exciting career option, it is imperative to consider the marketing aspects of your venture.

The ability to promote and sell your product/service, i.e., marketing is the key to succeed in any self-employment venture. So, a market survey should be considered as the first and foremost step in exploring the viability of your proposed venture, because marketing is all about generating revenue, the lifeline and ultimate objective of any business concern. Here our intention is not to make a formal marketing plan. The objective is just to activate your thought process to assess the viability of your chosen career. It is merely an attempt to objectively justify your choice, as well as enable you to take stock of your special skills and fortes so that you can suitably upgrade your skills, wherever considered necessary.

Understanding the Business Scene

We have already discussed some preparatory steps with the purpose of priming yourself for the prospective career change. You have also adequately analysed and explored your strengths vis-à-vis available career opportunities. So, by now you may be ready with your business concept and looking forward to start your new venture. After all the analysis and cross-examination, your decision just deserves an encouraging endorsement. But as you are aware career change is a big decision and career shift to self-employment is a much bigger decision, wherein higher risks and rewards are at stake. In view of this, it is desirable to adopt a very cautious and clever approach before you commit yourself. Remember the lessons learnt at this stage will come handy when you decide to plough a lonely furrow in your chosen venture.

Scrutinizing and reflecting on your new venture will not only improve your chances of success, but will also help you to constructively create your business plan and efficiently execute it. Keep in mind that you are going to invest substantial finance, time and energy on your new venture. So, you need to mull over some basic facts and challenges again in order to thwart the negative factors and thrive on the positive factors. The objective is merely to re-acquaint you with the cold realities of the business world, and not to dampen your spirits. Here, our objective is not to impart the professional expertise, but to give a ringside view of the business jungle to enable you to take informed and well-considered career decisions.

The following factors will provide you some practical pointers to identify and manage the risk factors aptly, so as to supplement your success potential. That is why you ought to think through your decision wisely with reference to the following pointers, before we proceed to discuss a formal business plan.

Appreciating Success Prospects

The survival rate of new ventures is really discouraging, as more than eighty percent of all new ventures pack up within five years. We may find it difficult to digest this data, especially when we come across so many new ventures flourishing everywhere. It is true that many new ventures are thriving and creating ever more possibilities; however, they are also creating a delusory illusion of success for many beginners. Unfortunately, it is also true that seven out of ten new ventures fail in the initial stages, closing down even before breaking even, and thus suffer financial losses over and above the opportunity costs and emotional setbacks. Even so, we do not take enough notice of so many failures because we see a little about the closed ventures.

These statistics paint a grim picture, which can potentially undermine a budding entrepreneur's confidence. And these bleak findings are not from the dubious sources. So, they do not have any convincing counterarguments. What's more, several credible sources validate the statistics, wherein the business failures outnumber the success stories by a huge margin. But then, my personal empirical experience rather suggests inverse proportion of the failures that is two out of five. And it is not that the sample size, comprising largely of my business acquaintances, is too small to reflect a reasonably true and fair picture. Nevertheless, it is not a representative sample, as it is purely based on my accumulated experiences and is not a standard survey of the entire population. On the other hand, it does indicate something more important and relevant, i.e., the success rate is a function of the socio-economic class, as well as an entrepreneur's personal profile. And the employed executives are definitely at the higher end of the social hierarchy and their profiles indubitably deserve a privileged position in the pecking order. Therefore, their success scope in the business cannot be compared with the universal ratios. However, at the end of the day, it is important to minimize such adverse odds whatever may be the failure rate. In view of that, we need to discuss the following issues, which are primarily responsible for the majority of business failures.

Resources: Most businesses fail because promoters fall short of resources in the critical stages of the business building. Unreasonable sanguinity can prompt you to start a business on a shoestring, but that makes it vulnerable in the infancy stages. So, you need to rightly assess the capital and other resources required at least to cross the break-even stage. Besides, you should have fifty percent extra funds as reserve to sustain you through the arduous start up period. Similarly, you need to determine other necessary resources required for your new venture and ensure that their paucity does not become a hindrance to the growth of your business. However, it does not imply that ample resources are mandatory to succeed in business. Remember, the self-made entrepreneurs always occupy most of the top slots in the richest people lists.

Early Success: Surprisingly, many enterprises fail as a result of easy and early success. There is no denying that such a success is a positive achievement. However, such a rapid growth is usually accompanied by a unique set of challenges. Just as you get more than the anticipated success in the early stages of your venture, you are likely to cope with many complex as well as rudimentary issues relating to the day-to-day management. In addition, you are supposed to lead your organization through unchartered territories. Obviously, many such issues cannot be foreseen at the time of preparing the business plan and as such, you will not have any contingency plans to deal with these challenges. Furthermore, when it is not easy to handle the planned affairs, how one can be expected to aptly manage the unexpected things.

However, you can sustain this sort of upturn if you have sufficient resources, viz. money, men, materials and machines at your disposal and know how to manage them. Your early success cannot overwhelm or intimidate you if you are adept at organizing human resources and know how to adeptly delegate. Rather, these two important keys will help you to build on the early success. And then, you can successfully navigate a thriving business by limiting your role in the executive operations and concentrating more on the high-level decision-making tasks.

Mentor: All successful entrepreneurs have one thing in common. They have good mentors to fall back on for guidance and criticism. You should earnestly solicit the guidance of a mentor, who can coach you what it takes to become a successful entrepreneur. You ought to seek their counsel on all important decisions in order to effectively harness their wisdom in realizing your entrepreneurial goals. But, do not just seek positive affirmations; rather be wary of any positive affirmations. Most good mentors are very particular about the negative aspects or risk factors that require more attention than the positive aspects. Usually, good mentors are good at putting across upsetting facts tactfully. However, occasionally they can be irritatingly opinionated particularly on such business decisions, where we are not comfortable. But we must bear in mind that they have our best interests in mind, which prompt them to direct us, challenge us, prod us, and even rebuke us to correct us. They make us think twice about the high-risk decisions, as they can clearly see some signs, which may not be clear to us. So, we ought to take full advantage of good mentors and finalize all strategic issues with their consent so as to maximize our prospects.

An important part of the secret of success in business is to maintain an optimum level of optimism at all stages. However, human nature is such that enthusiasm and interest in any new venture fades, as the impact of initial stimuli wears out. Here also, a mentor can play a positive part to keep us in the right gears and on our toes.

Partnership: Many businesses do not fail, but the partnerships managing them fail. When the alliance responsible for the management of business withers, business loses direction and drifts to failure. Behaviours of partners differ significantly in the pre-launch and post-launch periods, because gradually initial enthusiasm dwindles and the hard reality dawns. And then, the differences of opinion take its toll on the business. Personality conflict is the leading causative factor leading to the failed partnerships even between family members. More often than not, this and other fallible attributes of the human nature upsets the alliance and then focus shifts from managing the business to other non-productive squabbles and skirmishes.

Human nature is highly sensitive and susceptible to selfish motives. It further suffers from our inability or unwillingness to accept others views rationally and impartially. While forging a partnership, we habitually view more of positive factors and a rosy future. In the beginning, we hardly ever realize and prepare for the negative factors that usually crop up afterwards and catch us by surprise. In this backdrop, our dreams, desires, whims, fancies, egos, and self-willed attitudes take over our behaviour, which in turn takes its toll on the business alliance and eventually on the business. On the other hand, if we behave as responsible and mature individuals in the pre- and post-commencement phases of the business, we will not only sustain our partnership, but will also benefit from it in our business endeavours.

Family: We know that our family plays a crucial role in our career journey. And the family support is supposed to work in favour of any career endeavour. It not only helps to accelerate our career progress, but also rally round to establish the vital work-life balance in our life.

But then, it is paradoxical that the family is also a contributing factor for many business failures, either owing to lack of family support or due to gratuitous interference by the family members in the business affairs. And both the contradictory factors rather make entrepreneurs' life busier, not easier. Many businesses suffer because of the hectic lifestyles of the promoters involving professional plus personal chores. And many entrepreneurs attribute their business failure to the otiose and uncalled-for interference by their family members. Many studies validate this allegation, and it is not easy to rightly define the right role of family in the business operations. Furthermore, it is really difficult to determine the extent of family support that is beneficial for the business because, the issues involved are very personal and vary widely from case to case.

Therefore, entrepreneurs are supposed to wisely decide the role of their family in their business operations. Though separating family matters and business issues seems rather unworkable, it is a good idea. After examining the viability and workable extent of this passive yet positive approach in your case, you should decide direct and indirect role of all your family members in your business to ensure the smooth functioning of your business and optimum work-life balance in your life. And most importantly, make sure that everyone pays heed to it. Such an arrangement will make work and life easier and enjoyable for all the family members as well as boosts the prospects of your business. Lastly, entrepreneurs should appreciate the family concerns and family members need to appreciate the demanding task of starting a business.

New Trends: Technology is getting outdated faster than ever. And keeping with it requires us to be on our toes. In order to succeed in a business venture, an entrepreneur ought to be always aware of new business concepts and new technologies.

So, you have to constantly monitor how new trends will influence your line of work. You have to be ready all the time to change course along the lines of clear emerging trends, so as to cash in on the newer opportunities. Bear in mind that merely managing your enterprise to the best of your potential may not adequately protect you from the likely setbacks imposed by the external adverse trends. So, analysing newer trends should be regarded as an on ongoing function of your business.

I recall the case of a friend who left her job to undertake an educational cassettes creating and retailing enterprise. She achieved better than anticipated success, despite several routine hiccups, thanks to her enthusiasm for her newfound passion. However, she could not keep up with the latest in her business domain, as she used to be engrossed in the mundane affairs of her firm. So, she failed to acknowledge the threat from the high-technology sunrise mediums. She stubbornly clung to her tried, but static ways. And by the time she acknowledged the relevance and importance of the contemporary trends, it was too late to change the track, because many competitors had taken the first mover advantage to capture the market thanks to their economical and advanced products.

Besides, the ever-changing dynamics of the world of business demands a dynamic and proactive approach to the term passé. We have to actively guard that our business concept is aligned with the latest market trends and is not vulnerable to turning passé, which is no more even a slightly passive term.

Your assiduous performance is important to make it in the business; however, it will not take you to your goal if you do not recognize and capitalize on the newer opportunities. Unless seized, an opportunity is merely a floating fish in a school that is a chance. Therefore, you need to constantly read the signs and reflect on the latest trends. Most importantly, heed them to maintain your competitive edge. It is very important to survive and thrive in the modern world of business.

Planning Against a Business Failure

One has to be ruthless to take up the topic of business failure, when a budding entrepreneur is bursting with enthusiasm and optimism. On the other hand, it is very important to prepare you well for the contingencies if things do go wrong. It is imperative to mull over potential negative factors now because you will not have enough time once you take the plunge. At this juncture, dilly-dallying, particularly over the negative factors, is a self-destructive option. Besides, it can be counter-productive to examine these factors after committing yourself because then you will be too occupied to manage the demanding affairs of a start-up. And you should bear in mind that your successful service career does not guarantee your success as an entrepreneur.

It is certainly better to miss the boat than to sink the ship. You cannot afford to play the titanic game with your career. It is very important to learn the trade secrets before you commit. It will help you to effectively counter the adverse factors in order to prevent failure in your venture. Preventing business failure involves assessing the probable risk factors so as to make sure that adequate preventive measures are built into your business plan, as well as your psyche. So, before you take the plunge, you must plan against all overt and covert reasons of business failure. The following table lists some common and avertable causes of business failures. You can add a few personal and pertinent risk factors on your own. Next, you should assess your risk perception against each factor and accordingly decide a suitable averting strategy for the really risky factors. Here are some directions to finalize your strategy to deal with the probable causes of business failure.

You need to assess all risk factors on a scale of +2 to -2 where +2 = very favourable, +1 = favourable, 0 = neutral /unsure, - 1 = adverse and -2 = very adverse. Alternatively, you can just record your self-assessed risk ratings in the second column just against the pertinent risk factors. And then, you should brainstorm over all the negative entries in order to devise a suitable averting strategy to control the probable risk factors. Brainstorming involves analysing and synthesizing the risk factors. Here, analysis implies braking down the risk factor and synthesis implies combining the analysed parts to facilitate a suitable coping strategy. Simply put, take apart your risk factor and then strategically reassemble them to make them ineffective. You should also incorporate adverse and very adverse entries in your business plan along with a specific action plan to manage the vulnerable factors.

Planning against Business Failures Worksheet

Business Failure Factors	Your Rating	Averting Strategy
Unrealistic Vision		
Lacking Management Skills		
Poor Planning/No Planning		
Lacking Relevant Competence		
Insufficient Market Knowledge		
Inadequate Capital/Other Resources		
Inadequate Family Support		
Lack of Optimism		
Too Much Optimism/ Pessimism		
Lack of Focus/Momentum		
Lack of Work-Life Balance		
Underestimating Competition		
Plenty of Capital		
Prone to Money Mismanagement		
Inadequate Commitment to the Venture		
….		

Before you create a formal business plan, try to make these probable causes of business failure your stepping-stones to success. It is not very difficult. On the other hand, it is an opportunity because these risk factors impact everyone and the one who gets the better of these usually wins the game.

These factors are not insurmountable for a strong-willed person. An open and enabling mindset will help you to compete successfully. If you find a specific risk factor unwieldy, figure out a way to either manage it or hedge it. Think through some 'what if' and 'comparison' questions as well to gain confidence. In addition, have a contingency plan in place. This will supplement your risk-taking potential as well as risk managing ability. Remember, managing a business is all about managing risks, and risks are not limited to financial risks. Other equally, perhaps more important risks can have serious consequences on the emotional wellbeing, relationships, and above all self-esteem.

There are also some minor risks such as loss of our time and exertion, but then we may appreciate or not, in a way, they are rather enlightening and recompensing factors. In fact, these misperceived risks save us from other bigger risks. Then again, for a talented and ambitious person, there are some other equally important risks such as lost opportunities and opportunity costs of not starting a business. After appreciating the risks of starting a business, as well as, not starting a business, we take up the process of creating a generic business plan.

Planning your Business Plan

After understanding the causes of business failures and scrutinizing the relevant ones, we move to the most important step in starting a business, i.e., creating a business plan. A business plan is a simulation of a business idea. It is a sort of testing laboratory to test the feasibility of a business concept under consideration. In other words, it is preconceiving a business idea from the concept stage to the commissioning stage. A rational, realistic and thorough business plan is the key to prevent a business failure. The old saying, "People do not plan to fail, they fail to plan" truly reflects the connection between planning and business failures.

A business plan is like a car's headlight that shows the road ahead. It gives you an opportunity to learn business by experiencing business. Business is a risky endeavour, and any oversight could cost you dearly in terms of money, time and emotional setbacks. Your business plan gives you a chance to hone your business skills.

Preparation of a business plan takes a lot of time, energy and money in the process of gathering relevant data, researching, evaluating core idea, analysing market and reflecting on your business concept. Your business plan will collate inputs from all your preparations in order to give a representative picture of your prospective venture in a prescriptive framework. All this investment is worth it as it preempts detrimental mistakes at the execution stage. Planning process is also a very educative experience, as it makes you familiar with the business processes before you invest your precious capital. And it is far easier and economical to deal with a problem at the planning stage than to confront it in your real business. That is why the planning process is as important as the product i.e. business plan.

So, you should take active part in the making of your business plan. This exposure provides a useful grounding since it lets you foresee and solve the problems with the least effort.

Here we intend to discuss a generic business plan keeping in mind the usual requirements of a standard business enterprise. However, you need to tailor it to suit your strong suit in addition to other personal and business needs. Remember, each business plan is unique in view of the unique set of variables influencing that particular business and your personal factors. You should not expect a readymade business plan to meet your requirements. There cannot be a standard business plan, which completely conforms to your specific needs. However, business plans relating to your intended business activity and somewhat corresponding to your personal parameters can help you further explore the venture as well as guide you in making your plan. But it cannot qualify as your business plan.

Creating your Business Plan

Understanding the process of creating a business plan will give you many meaningful insights on your business idea and the ways to start, manage, and expand it. It will certainly increase the success potential of your proposed venture. Here is a standard structure of a business plan followed by a brief explanation of each module. Remember the following modules represent general guidelines; you can change or modify them in any way that best suits you and your line of business.

A Standard Business Plan Outline

>> Plan Summary

>> Business Model— Business Idea & Concept, Products & Services, Ownership & Organization

>> Personal Factors— Aspirations, Expertise, Needs, and Resources

>> Preparatory Steps

>> Operational Plan

>> Business Outlook— Opportunities and Threats

>> The Appendix

Plan Summary: The Business Plan summary should concisely explain the business proposal. This should include everything that you would like to cover in a brief interview to introduce your proposed venture. Here are some important items that your plan summary should include:

> The vision & mission statements
> Promoters' particulars
> Products/ services offered
> Business location
> Market/customer information
> Capital required
> Staffing plans
> Industry outlook
> Promoters' long-term plans

Though business plan summary is the first and most important section in your plan, it is usually finalized after everything else because most subsequent sections will have a bearing on it. To begin with, you can make a rough draft to serve as a reference point while covering other functional sections of your plan.

Business Model— Business Idea & Concept, Products & Services, Ownership & Organization

Business Idea and Concept: Here you have to briefly define your basic business idea. You should explain how it will work as a commercial concept in a competitive market. This section should also address the following queries.

• What is your business philosophy?
• What are the market needs you are targeting?
• How do you plan to satisfy these needs?
• What are your competitive advantages? Justify it with your major strengths.
• What is special about your business concept compared to direct and indirect competitors?

Products and Services: This section details what are your products and/or services and why you have selected these. Here, you are supposed to describe your products and/or services in detail along with relevant photos, technical specifications, drawings, patents/copyright information, pricing, key features, sales brochures, etc. primarily from the prospective customers' perspective. If your offerings list is quite large, here just describe groups of products/services stressing the general benefits to potential customers. However, you can append the bulky details, like market surveys, promotional materials and any other relevant, but voluminous information in the appendix section. But here you must incorporate all the strategic aspects of your offerings clearly touching on their strong points plus a comparative analysis of your products/services with reference to the competition.

You should also very briefly mention how a particular product/service line relates to your personal profile, particularly work values and interests inventory, as well as how making a career in this line will help you realize your long-term vision. It is very important to establish the compatibility of the proposed line with your long-term career vision at this stage, because you will considerably lose your flexibility to revise your career vision after commencing operations.

Ownership & Organization: This section deals with the legal form of ownership and the management style to run the proposed venture. Legal form of ownership depends on your business type, size, funding requirements and your personal preferences. Career changers normally prefer sole proprietorship or partnership in the beginning and move up to the limited liability Company when they are ready to share ownership with others to source finance.

Organization part is meant to describe the management style and working of your organization, i.e., who is responsible for what in your organization. Usually, an organization chart is used to describe the organization structure of the firm. It clearly describes all the important positions and accompanying responsibilities. It is important to add a narrative description to the organization chart along with the profiles of the individuals manning all the important positions. In essence, you have to demonstrate how your team complements your expertise to make a formidable company to take on the competition head-on. This exercise will not only make you clear-headed on the working of your organization, but also reflect on your preparedness in the eyes of potential investors, employees and other business associates as well as give them confidence about your venture.

The management style section is supposed to briefly discuss the work culture of the firm. It should also highlight whether management controls are system based or individual based and how authority along with accountability moves throughout the organization. You should also delineate how you intend to make the organization bigger than you. Only an organization not limited by an individual's potential can optimally leverage the current business opportunities and capitalize on the future opportunities to grow.

Personal Factors — Aspirations, Expertise, Needs, and Resources

This part deals with your individual attributes and how they relate to the project under consideration. It primarily elaborates on the following issues.

- How your professional and personal aspirations relate to the project?
- What core competency and expertise do you personally bring to your business enterprise?
- What personal role do you define for you in the venture in the near term— say three years? Also, state what role you foresee for yourself in the medium term (3-10 years) as well as in the long term (after 10 years). If you do not wish to commit yourself for a long haul, specify your succession plans.
- How this project can fulfil your personal needs— professional, financial, emotional and others?
- How your family members and friends relate to the venture? Is there any conflict between your family commitments/priorities   vis-à-vis   your   business obligations?
- Do you want to make it a sole proprietorship/ partnership/family business or a separate corporate entity? And why?

- Whether your financial and other resources are sufficient to sail you through the break-even level of the project. If not, what are your alternative arrangements?
- How prepared are you to endure the consequences if things do not move as per your plan?

Preparatory Steps: All pre-operational activities necessary to start the project are covered in this module. This step is very important for the reason that many decisions taken at this stage have a direct bearing on the success of the venture. What's more, these measures cannot be easily reversed. So, it is imperative to wisely plan all the steps required to provide a strong foundation to your business. Some common preoperational steps include organizing registration formalities, finalizing location, arranging finance, setting up infrastructure, and arranging equipment, technology, and suchlike paraphernalia. Making a business plan is also an important preparatory step, which attempts to conceive and perceive the preoperational as well as operational aspects on paper to get a believable and dependable feel of the venture.

Operational Plans: Proper planning is important to ensure smooth functioning in any endeavour, but more so in a business enterprise. Operational plans provide an overview of the future working and status of the business so as to facilitate an optimal alignment and coordination of the various functions of the business to maximize profit, profitability and other enterprise goals.

In a business, accelerating all the functions in a coordinated manner at the right velocity is a challenge. Here operational plans help you to foresee the expected performance of various functions and adopt appropriate corrective measures in the wanting areas so as to ensure overall optimum performance. You can use flexible planning in tandem with 'What if' analysis to identify the gaps, which can be properly plugged by suitably tweaking the plans. Operational plans cover all the important functions of a business. For example - marketing plan, personnel plan, utilities plan, production plan, financial plan, and so on.

Business Outlook — Opportunities and Threats

Often the challenge and excitement of running a new business keeps budding entrepreneurs fully engrossed in routine rigmarole. While the going is good or tough, they tend to overlook the future outlook of the business. In fact, it is equally important to regularly explore the probable future opportunities and threats so as to thrive and survive in the business. Making business outlook review a distinct part of your business plan encourages you to constantly explore and seize the credible opportunities as well as positively deal with the probable threats. Besides, it gives confidence to other stakeholders about the continuity of the venture. Periodically, thinking about business outlook provides a great stimulus to not only raise the bar, but to achieve it as well.

The Appendix: All detailed documents, information and other records, which can clutter or dilute the focus from the relevant point, should be appended here. Some common contents of this section are:

- Products and/or services detailed description, including product drawings/pictures/brochures/blueprints/ tech. specifications, details of market surveys, letters of encouragement from potential customers
- Promoters and key executives resumes, list of business advisors, detailed organization charts
- Legal documents like — licenses, patents, copies of leases, building permits, other contracts
- Maps of location, building layout and blueprints, detailed lists of equipment, machinery and other paraphernalia
- Financial figures, prospective financial data, and personal credit history
- Industry studies and any other information backing the assumptions in the business plan

Monitoring the Plan: You need to periodically review your business plan. If required, revise it in line with the current needs and contemporary trends. A flexible and progressive approach to your business plan along with a willingness to change it, if the situation demands, is necessary to keep it a winning document.

Usually entrepreneurs do not give adequate emphasis to the monitoring activity in their business plan, which is merely viewed as a feasibility assessment document of a business start-up. However, ensuring continuity of a business is also important to make a business viable on an on-going basis. And sensibly monitoring your plan will help you achieve that. Moreover, it gives a positive impression about the promoter's long-term commitment to the project to various stakeholders. Investors also differentiate between the genuine promoters and fly-by-night operators on the basis of their long-term commitment to the project. Such commitment can be demonstrated with a willingness to constantly monitor the operations in an attempt to ensure continued growth. Therefore, you should make it a part of your plan and briefly discuss the monitoring scheme to be followed during the project implementation stage as well as after the commencement of the operations. The monitoring scheme should facilitate that all the requisite modifications are incorporated in the respective parts as well as the plan summary at pre-defined intervals to secure your business goals.

The above-mentioned business plan is a generic one, outlining the basic steps common to most businesses. Though your business plan will broadly move along the lines of above-mentioned steps, it will be only one of its kinds, because your personal factors as well as business activity, size, location, market, and suchlike factors will determine its final shape. It will be an interesting and easier exercise once you incorporate your contents in the plan modules to reflect your specific requirements. What's more, it is not supposed to be a static document in the strict sense; it should change corresponding to any change in the underlying factors. However, it is supposed to keep the ultimate goal in focus all the time.

Remember that you are the best person to decide most of the inputs to your business plan, especially personal factors. So, you should strive to make your business plan yourself. You may involve your well-informed friends or your business mentor in the process. In any case, do not forget to get it scrutinized from your mentor or an informed friend, who can review it rationally and realistically. Never ever attempt to implement your plan without getting a second opinion from a reliable source. However, if you further require any help, you should seek professional guidance from a qualified and experienced professional in an attempt to refine and vet your plan. And if you find it difficult to make your plan or get it properly reviewed, you may contact us for further guidance.

There is no formula or magic potion to guarantee your success in a business. However, you can improve your chances of success by following various points discussed here before. In view of the importance and relevance of these guidelines, here we again list a few main points to enable you to assess your preparations.

✓ Starting business for the right reasons
✓ Positivism and perseverance
✓ Rightly researching and reasonably reflecting on your business concept
✓ Drafting a good business plan
✓ Right assessment of market potential
✓ Properly profiling the target customers
✓ Right assessment of resources required
✓ Flexible attitude and adept at adopting to changes
✓ Making best use of information and resources

Often our misperceived 'busy-ness in career' induce us to procrastinate by taking shelter in the self-induced time constraints, which not only comes in the way of our 'career business', but also intimidates our 'career in business.' First, procrastination can come in the way of timely start of our venture, which merely delays the realization of our professional vision. After that, it can come in the way of timely monitoring of our business plans, which can actually deprive us the chance to make it big in the business.

We must keep in mind that planning for business is not a one-time affair. A business demands dynamic attention and continuous monitoring of various factors affecting it. And the business model and management style ought to evolve and change as business considerations change. A business plan is a worthy device so long as one remembers it is not an end in itself. So, ongoing business planning, flexible approach and active management can substantially improve your chances of success in a business venture.

9. Take Charge

Your career is your responsibility. Your career decisions are your prerogative. And you owe it to yourself to manage your career optimally. In fact, here you are the boss. You have to make the big decisions yourself.

Will you accept this challenge? Will you take charge of your career and do whatever it takes to reach your full potential?

Finding your dream job is not difficult. But it demands perseverance and commitment. Remember, it is one thing to be inspired, quite another to be inspired by the idea of being inspired. When your enthusiasm is at its peak, it is natural to rush headlong. The impulse is to just take the plunge. But if you think through and analyze first, you will be able to design the right career plan. So, you should make sure that your game plan should not merely have the elements that fit the frame you use to see your professional identity. It should not become a mere delivery mechanism for your pre-conceived notions.

How you view a situation largely determines its outcome. A positive and proactive attitude is a prerequisite to view your options and future clearly. Your career plan is a function of many variables, personal and external. Thinking over it properly will help you to put in place a holistic approach towards your career objectives. And that will encourage you to adopt systematic and proactive career management practices instead of ad-hoc and reactive practices.

This resource is intended to help you to appreciate a bigger picture of your career. It forces you to look at the big picture, not a part of the frame, so that your action plan and the resulting execution regimen are based on the 360-degree view. This panoptic view will help you to see the future clearly. And this clarity will bring value and meaning to your life. It will no longer be a predicament to predict your career destination.

When all is said and done, it is your duty to tap your full potential. No one else can do it for you. Career planning can make you career conscious. It can put you in the driver's seat. It can show you the way forward. It can help you to accelerate your journey to your dream job. But, it demands initiative from your side. You have to steer your way to your dream career.

So, take charge. Success awaits you. Good luck!